Cakes & Pastries

OLIVIA ERSCHEN
Writer and Food Stylist

SUSAN LAMMERS
Editor

LINDA HINRICHS
CAROL KRAMER
Designers

PATRICIA BRABANT
Photographer

SUSAN MASSEY–WEIL
Prop Stylist

EDITH ALLGOOD
Illustrator

D1374252

CALIFORNIA
CULINARY
ACADEMY

Ortho Books

Publisher
Robert L. Iacopi

Editorial Director
Min S. Yee

Managing Editors
Jim Beley
Anne Coolman
Susan Lammers
Michael D. Smith
Sally W. Smith

Production Director
Ernie S. Tasaki

Editors
Richard H. Bond
Alice E. Mace

System Manager
Christopher Banks

System Consultant
Mark Zielinski

Asst. System Managers
Linda Bouchard
William F. Yusavage

Photographic Director
Alan Copeland

Photographers
Laurie A. Black
Richard A. Christman

Asst. Production Manager
Darcie S. Furlan

Associate Editor
Jill Fox

Production Editors
Don Mosley
Anne Pederson

Chief Copy Editor
Rebecca Pepper

Photo Editors
Kate O'Keeffe
Pam Peirce

National Sales Manager
Charles H. Aydelotte

Sales Associate
Susan B. Boyle

Operations Assistant
Gail L. Davis

Administrative Assistant
Georgiann Wright

Address all inquiries to
Ortho Books
Chevron Chemical Company
Consumer Products Division
575 Market Street
San Francisco, CA 94105

Copyright © 1985
Chevron Chemical Company
All rights reserved under
international and Pan-American
copyright conventions.

First Printing in July, 1985

1 2 3 4 5 6 7 8 9
85 86 87 88 89 90

ISBN 0-89721-059-X

Library of Congress Catalog Card
Number 85-070884

Chevron Chemical Company
575 Market Street, San Francisco, CA 94105

Danielle Walker *(left)* is chairman of the board and founder of the California Culinary Academy. **Olivia Erschen** *(right)* trained as a pastry chef with Jean Bertranou, former chef and owner of the famed restaurant L'Ermitage in Los Angeles. Since that time Olivia has traveled extensively throughout the United States, France, and Italy developing her pastry-making expertise. In addition, she has taught many classes in pastry making for both professionals and nonprofessionals, has worked as a food consultant and food stylist, and has published articles in *Bon Appétit*.

The California Culinary Academy Among the forefront of American institutions leading the culinary renaissance in this country, the California Culinary Academy in San Francisco has gained a reputation as one of the most outstanding professional chef training schools in the world. With a teaching staff recruited from the best restaurants of Western Europe, the California Culinary Academy educates students from around the world in the preparation of classical cuisine. The recipes in this book were created in consultation with the Academy's chefs.

Acknowledgments

Recipe Consultants
Rita Leinwand
Judy Pacht
Mickey Erschen
Gloria Bowers
Carol Cole

Food Styling Assistants
Kathy Briggs
Carol Cole
Gloria Bowers
Carolyn Vaughan

Photographers
Laurie Black, Academy photography
Fischella, photograph of
    Danielle Walker
Michael Lamotte, back cover

Food Styling for Back Cover
Amy Nathan

Food Styling at the Academy
Jeff Van Hanswyk

Color Separations
Balzer-Shopes

Calligraphy
Chuck Wertman

Editorial Assistants
Anne Ardillo
Bil Lawrence

Special Thanks To

Arthur Wells
Courtney Flavin
Juanita Erschen
Pauli Moss
Med McComb

Jean Bertranou
Rosalie Grant
Mary Erschen
Eric Fombonne
Yves Thuries

Front Cover

For the lightest confection imaginable, try Chocolate Mousse Cake (page 48). Decorate with fresh strawberries and Chantilly Cream.

Back Cover Photos

Upper left: Leeks, carrots, potatoes, onions, garlic, and herbs are just some of the ingredients that go into a rich veal stock.

Upper right: Two trouts garnished with lemon and parsley are ready to enter the fish poacher, where they will be simmered in white wine and herbs.

Lower left: Four Cornish game hens are arranged on a platter with baby carrots and green beans.

Lower right: Rosettes of whipped cream are piped onto a cake with a pastry bag and an open-star tip.

C O N T E N T S

Cakes & Pastries

Beaten egg whites are carefully folded into a chocolate cake batter to lighten it before baking. A large bowl is essential for proper folding.

Cake & Pastry Basics

Faces light up, voices lift, and eyes sparkle when a cake or pastry enters our midst. The sweet tastes, luscious textures, and striking appearances make these delectable creations among the most favored foods in the world. In fact, they have come to symbolize abundance, celebration, happiness, and well-being. Here we teach you the basics as well as the secrets for preparing perfect cakes and pastries.

THE BEST OF FRENCH AND AMERICAN BAKING TRADITIONS

Baking cakes and pastries is one of the most satisfying and enjoyable ways to put your creative powers to work in the kitchen. The recipes developed for this book expand upon the creative tradition of cakes and pastries by combining the baking traditions of both France and America to give a new twist to old favorites. Old-fashioned Hubbard squash pie filling is baked in a freestanding fluted tart shell instead of the traditional pie crust (see page 83). French puff pastry shells hold old-fashioned vanilla custard topped with a raspberry-rhubarb compote (see page 90). Many recipes, however, remain distinctly American or thoroughly French. All of the French recipes have been adapted to use ingredients found in the United States and are easily produced in the American kitchen. You are sure to find the ideal cake or pastry for any occasion, whether it is a simple family supper or an elegant holiday gathering.

As an additional aid to the baker, the last steps of almost every recipe provide detailed information on how to decorate and present the cakes and pastries in ways that will make them appear really special and professional. These finishing touches will take your creations beyond the ordinary. It's well worth your time to put forth the extra effort required, but if you don't have the time or inclination, your cake or pastry will still taste as wonderful with a simple presentation.

Each chapter begins with useful information on the easiest way to make each type of pastry.

Step-by-step photographs or illustrations are provided to help the novice baker understand the basic recipes and techniques. In general, each chapter proceeds from easy recipes to ones that are more complicated. This chapter, *Cake and Pastry Basics*, will be your reference throughout the rest of the book. It guides you in selecting the right pastry for the occasion, the equipment needed for baking, and useful information on baking ingredients and techniques. This chapter also contains tips on high-altitude baking and an ingredients substitution chart. Refer to the back of the book for a glossary of baking terms.

THE ROLE OF PASTRY IN A MEAL

The perfect cake or pastry provides just the right taste to round out the meal, leaving your guests with a happy sense of completion. If the dessert does not complement the preceding dishes well, a meal that was otherwise perfectly fine might end on a bad note. Take the time beforehand to think through the entire menu and plan to serve an appropriate cake or pastry. Don't simply make a dessert that you know you can make well without giving thought to how it fits into the meal. It is just as important to select a pastry that suits the meal and the occasion as it is to make it well and present it attractively. The guidelines below will help you choose the ideal dessert.

☐ After a heavy, rich meal, serve a light, refreshing dessert such as cookies and sorbet.

☐ After a spicy meal, serve a cool, refreshing dessert (such as citrus fruit, fruit Bavarian, sorbet, ice cream, custard, or frozen parfait).

☐ After a simple, light meal, a heavy or rich dessert can be served (chocolate layer cake with ice cream, for example).

☐ Do not repeat in the dessert textures and flavors that appear in the meal (for example, do not serve tart lemon meringue pie after lemon chicken; do not serve an egg-and-cream-based dessert after a meal with an egg-and-cream-sauced entrée). The dessert should provide a pleasant contrast to the meal that precedes it.

☐ Avoid serving a dessert with the same pastry crust as the entrée (do not serve puff pastry tarts after salmon in puff pastry or beef Wellington; do not serve a pie after quiche, and so forth).

☐ Creamy-textured desserts are best after a meal of roasted meat, vegetables, and salad.

☐ Serve a dessert that suits the meal, the occasion, and the group you are serving. The decoration and presentation of a dessert can make it more or less appropriate for various occasions. Serve a portion that suits the people you are serving. Individual puff pastries filled with fresh raspberries, custard, and crème fraîche are perfect for a four-course dinner party, but not for a country picnic. For picnics and casual buffet dinners, it's best to serve cakes and pastries that keep well at room temperature, can be transported and served in their baking pans, and are easy to cut and eat (such as bundt and pound cakes, sheet cakes, cupcakes, pies, and tarts).

HOW TO MEASURE INGREDIENTS

Measure each ingredient carefully and precisely, as indicated in the recipe's ingredients list. All recipe measurements are for level cups, teaspoons, or tablespoons unless otherwise indicated. When a mold is buttered and floured before baking, this butter and flour is not included in the ingredients list. It is preferable to have one set of measuring utensils for wet ingredients and another set for dry ingredients.

To Measure Liquids Measure liquids in a standard glass or plastic measuring cup with a pouring spout. Place the cup on a level surface and read the measurement at eye level. Measuring cups are available in 1-cup, 2-cup, and 4-cup sizes.

To Measure Dry Ingredients
Measure in standard metal or plastic cups that hold exact capacities ($\frac{1}{4}$-cup, $\frac{1}{3}$-cup, $\frac{1}{2}$-cup, and 1-cup measures). Scoop the ingredient into the cup, pile it high, then level it off to rim of cup with flat knife.

To Measure Small Amounts Use standard measuring spoons for liquid or dry ingredients. Available in sets of four ($\frac{1}{4}$-teaspoon, $\frac{1}{2}$-teaspoon, 1-teaspoon, and 1-tablespoon sizes), stainless steel or plastic are best.

Flour, sugar, milk, butter, eggs, nuts, raisins, fruits, and spices are just some of the ingredients that are transformed into cakes, pies, tarts, and pastries of all sorts. Using the freshest ingredients obtainable is an important step in making fine cakes and pastries.

Good baking equipment makes baking easier and allows you to create a greater variety of cakes and pastries.

BAKING EQUIPMENT

The following is an extensive list and discussion of all the equipment—from appliances to utensils—useful for baking cakes and pastries.

Appliances All recipes in this book can be baked in either a gas or an electric oven. Test your oven at several different temperatures with an oven thermometer (the mercury type is best) to see if it is accurately calibrated. If it is off by 25° F or less, you can compensate by raising or lowering the oven temperature. If it is off by as much as 50° F, have your oven recalibrated. In a standard oven, bake pastries on the center rack unless otherwise directed. Leave 1 to 2 inches between pans, and between pans and walls of oven. Do not bake on more than one oven rack at a time; if you do, the goods baking on the bottom rack will tend to burn because they are close to the heating element and because heat will reflect from the pan on the upper shelf. Overfilling the oven causes uneven baking. You can bake any of the recipes in a convection oven, but you may need to adjust the oven temperature or baking time since convection ovens sometimes bake foods more rapidly than standard ovens. Avoid baking in microwave ovens; they generally bake unevenly and produce pale pastries.

In pastry making, doughs are frequently chilled in the refrigerator to relax gluten and firm up butter. These doughs should be refrigerated at 40° F. If you purchase a new refrigerator, choose one that has shelves large enough to accommodate your baking sheets and slab of marble.

The freezer should be separate from the refrigerator and have horizontal shelves. To freeze pastry for the maximum amount of time indicated, the freezer must maintain a temperature of 0° F or less at all times. Double-wrap all pastry goods in freezer material or place in rigid

Basics

BAKING TOOLS AND UTENSILS

The following is a list of tools and utensils useful in baking. Certainly you don't need everything in this list, but the better equipped you are, the easier baking will be. For descriptions of some of the less common items in the list see the glossary on pages 122–123.

Apple corer
Blue ice
Bulb baster
Colander
Comb scraper
Docker
Dough scrapers: metal, rubber, or plastic
Egg beater
Food mill
Funnel
Grater: hand or rotary
Juicer
Knives: chef's, paring, slicing, serrated, and matte knife; sharpening steel
Measuring cups
Measuring spoons
Mixing bowls: stainless steel, glass or ceramic, copper

Pastry bags, ornamenting tubes, coupling unit
Pastry blender
Pastry brushes
Pastry cutters
Pastry-cutting wheel
Peeler: vegetable peeler
Pie or cake server
Pie weights
Pitters
Putty knife
Rolling pins
Rulers
Scissors: kitchen shears
Scrapers: rubber, metal
Sieves
Sifters
Skewers: metal, wood
Spatulas
Spoons: wooden, slotted stainless steel
Storage containers
Strainers (sieves, sifters)
Thermometers: oven, freezer, refrigerator, instant-read, candy
Timer
Tongs
Wire whisks
Wooden spoons
Zester

Other disposable supplies:
Aluminum foil
Cardboard cake bases
Cheesecloth
Foil and paper cupcake liners
Kitchen parchment paper
Marking tape and pens
Paper lace doilies
Paper towels
Plastic bags
Plastic wrap
Waxed paper

PAN SUBSTITUTION CHART

Whenever possible, use the size and shape pan recommended in the recipe you are using. If you do not have the right size pan or wish to vary the shape, you can consult the chart below to find a reasonable substitute. Choose a pan that has the same volume and similar depth as the pan in the recipe. The depth may vary up to ½ inch as long as the volume remains the same. The volume of a pan is measured by the amount of liquid it holds when filled to the rim. (This does not refer to the amount of batter the pan holds.) You may need to bake your cake a little longer if you choose a deeper pan than the one recommended.

Pan Measurements

Sides x Depth	Shape of Pan	Volume of Pan
2¾"x1⅜"	muffin cups	scant ½ cup
4"x12"x2"	deerback (loaf)	1 quart (4 cups)
4½"x10½"x2½"	deerback (loaf)	1 quart (4 cups)
9"x1¼"	pie plate	1 quart (4 cups)
8"x1½"	round	1 quart (4 cups)
8"x8"x1½"	square	1½ quarts (6 cups)
7"x11"x2"	rectangular	1½ quarts (6 cups)
4½"x8½"x2½"	loaf	1½ quarts (6 cups)
10"x2"	deep-dish pie	1½ quarts (6 cups)
8"x2"	round	1½ quarts (6 cups)
9"x1½"	round	1½ quarts (6 cups)
8"x8"x2"	square	2 quarts (8 cups)
9"x9"x1½"	square	2 quarts (8 cups)
5"x9"x3"	loaf	2 quarts (8 cups)
9"x2"	round	2 quarts (8 cups)
9"x3"	bundt	2¼ quarts (9 cups)
8½"x3½"	Kugelhopf (tube)	2¼ quarts (9 cups)
8"x3¼"	tube	2¼ quarts (9 cups)
9"x9"x2"	square	2½ quarts (10 cups)
9½"x2½"	springform	2½ quarts (10 cups)
9"x13"x2"	rectangular	3 quarts (12 cups)
10"x2½"	springform	3 quarts (12 cups)
10"x3½"	bundt	3 quarts (12 cups)

lidded containers, try to force all air from around pastry, label, and date. See individual chapters for freezer tips for each type of pastry.

Recipes indicate when and how a food processor can be used to increase baking efficiency. It is most useful for mixing pastry dough, grinding nuts or crumbs, puréeing fruits, and creaming ingredients. It is not recommended for beating egg whites or whipping cream.

A stand-type electric mixer is an invaluable aid in pastry making. The best mixers are heavy and have a strong motor with three attachments: a whip, a paddle, and a bread hook. A deep, straight-sided bowl with a rounded bottom is easiest to use. If you bake frequently, invest in an extra whip and bowl. A portable electric mixer is a good supplement to the stand mixer because you can use it when the other mixer is in action or when you need to beat only a small amount. Buy a portable mixer with a strong motor and several speeds.

Rolling Pins and Work Surfaces If you can buy only one rolling pin, get either a heavy, wooden-handled one with ball bearings or a handleless straight wooden pin. The following three types are especially useful.

□ A heavy, hardwood American rolling pin with ball bearings, measuring 27 inches overall; used for rolling out yeast-risen doughs or puff pastry.

□ A heavy, straight, wooden French rolling pin without handles (17¾ inches long and 2 inches in diameter) for rolling out pie and tart doughs, cookie dough, puff pastry, and almond paste.

□ A tapered beechwood rolling pin without handles (20½ inches long, 1½ inches in diameter at center, and ⅞ inch in diameter at the ends) for rolling circular pieces of dough or small, thin pieces of dough; especially useful in obtaining even dough thickness.

Do not wash wooden rolling pins or soak them in water. Wipe off your rolling pin with a clean, soft cloth after every use.

Pastry can be rolled out on any clean, smooth, flat surface (marble, wood, laminated plastic, or acrylic). Polished marble is the ideal surface because it is smooth and easiest to chill. Use wood or durable acrylic cutting boards for cutting or chopping pastry. Always reserve one chopping board or one area of your chopping block for pastry only. Pastry should not be prepared on the same surface on which you cut onions, garlic, and other strongly flavored savories.

Pots and Pans Select pans one by one to suit your cooking needs (rather than buying a matching set). Choose heavy, thick-bottomed pans of nonreactive material that will conduct heat evenly over the entire bottom surface of the pan. Plain aluminum pans conduct heat well, but react with acidic foods to produce a metallic taste and often turn egg-yolk-based preparations gray. They can be used to heat nonacidic liquids. Stainless steel pans are nonreactive, but conduct heat poorly, causing thick mixtures to stick to the bottom and scorch. Stainless steel is good for heating liquids or poaching fruits in syrup. A large stainless steel pot is lightweight and easy to lift when filled with large quantities of heavy liquids and is therefore a valuable addition to your collection of pans. The pans should also have strong, riveted, ovenproof handles and tight-fitting lids.

Baking Sheets and Pans Select baking sheets and pans that are most suitable for your baking needs. Remember that some materials are good heat conductors and hold heat well while others reflect heat. Pans also vary considerably in their overall quality and thickness. Shiny metal pans reflect heat and produce pastries that are delicately browned and tender-crusted but are not very crisp. Dark metal, glass, or ceramic pans hold heat and produce deeply browned, thick-crusted, crisp pastries. Heavy aluminum, carbon steel or cast iron, glass, or ceramic pans conduct and hold heat well and can be used for most pastries.

Cake, cookie, and tart tins come in a variety of shapes and sizes. Clockwise from bottom: heart-shaped cake tin, fluted-edge tart and tartlet tins, loaf pans, scallop-edged tart tin, tart band, cookie cut-outs, Madeleine molds, Kugelhopfs, springform cake pan, brioche pans, and a deerback cake pan.

RECIPE MODIFICATION CHART FOR HIGH-ALTITUDE BAKING

Feet Above Sea Level	Reduce Each Teaspoon Baking Powder By	Reduce Each Cup Sugar By	Increase Each Cup Liquid By
3,000–5,000	⅛ teaspoon	1 tablespoon	2 tablespoons
5,000–7,000	⅛–¼ teaspoon	2 tablespoons	2–3 tablespoons
7,000–10,000	¼ teaspoon	2–3 tablespoons	3–4 tablespoons
Above 10,000	¼–½ teaspoon	2–3 tablespoons	3–4 tablespoons

Over 3,000 feet: Increase oven temperature by 25° F.
Underbeat eggs (beat whites to soft peak stage).

Over 10,000 feet: Add one extra egg and increase each cup flour by 1–2 tablespoons.

Baking sheets can be used to bake any freestanding pastry that does not take its shape from the pan (such as cream puff pastries, puff pastries, tarts baked in flan rings, cookies, and certain breads). Select a heavy (¹⁄₁₆ inch thick) baking sheet with a rim less than ½ inch high. Thin baking sheets buckle when placed in the oven and conduct heat poorly, producing uneven browning. If you wish to use nonstick baking sheets, purchase ones of heavy-gauge metal, coated with a top-quality nonstick material or glazed with silicone resin.

Try not to scratch the surface of baking sheets. Avoid scraping them with metal objects or abrasives. Season carbon steel pans with oil before their first use. To clean carbon steel and tinned steel pans, simply rinse with hot water and dry with a towel immediately, or simply wipe the pan clean with a soft, dry towel while the pan is still warm. This eventually produces a well-seasoned pan.

TEMPERATURE CHART

Altitude	Water Boils At:
Sea level	212° F
2,000 feet	208° F
5,000 feet	203° F
7,500 feet	198° F
10,000 feet	194° F
15,000 feet	185° F
30,000 feet	158° F

HIGH-ALTITUDE BAKING

At altitudes of over 3,000 feet, the lower air pressure causes cakes and pastries to bake differently. Water boils at a lower temperature, and it is harder to heat things; liquids evaporate more quickly; leavenings expand more; sugar becomes more concentrated; and batters have a greater tendency to stick to their pans.

To compensate for these differences, increase the cooking time for foods that are boiled, and raise the oven temperature for baked goods by 25° F. Increase liquids, decrease leavenings, underbeat eggs and egg-based batters, decrease sugar, and butter and flour pans well or line with nonstick parchment paper. Consult the charts above for exact recipe changes.

SUCCESSFUL BAKING

Your success in making cakes and pastries will be directly related to your approach. If you are well organized and ready when you begin, you will find pastry making a pleasure.

☐ Read through the entire recipe before you begin.

☐ Review any techniques with which you are not familiar.

☐ Assemble all of the equipment and ingredients. Use the ingredients recommended in the recipe.

☐ Measure all ingredients precisely and carefully.

☐ Prepare pans and preheat oven.

☐ Break the recipe into manageable steps to suit your schedule. Now you are ready to combine the ingredients as directed in the recipe.

Sometimes it is important that you combine ingredients rapidly, one after another (as for génoise), and you could not produce a good cake if you had to stop to measure out each ingredient as you proceeded with the recipe. Many baking errors can be avoided if you read the recipe before you start.

Remember, above all, that pastry making should always be fun! There are so many nice surprises—the magical way simple ingredients combine to produce doughs that rise to ten times their original height in the oven, or the way melted chocolate turns into a paper-thin chocolate ruffle on cold marble with just a few quick movements of the wrist. It is fun, even relaxing, to perform this magic under the right circumstances with the right equipment and ingredients.

EMERGENCY SUBSTITUTIONS CHART

Ingredient	Amount	Substitution
Baking powder	1 teaspoon	⅓ teaspoon baking soda plus ½ teaspoon cream of tartar
	1 teaspoon	¼ teaspoon baking soda plus ½ cup buttermilk or yogurt (to replace ½ cup liquid in recipe)
Butter	1 cup	⅞ cup lard
	1 cup	1 cup hydrogenated vegetable shortening
	1 cup	1 cup margarine
Buttermilk	1 cup	1 cup yogurt
	1 cup	1 cup sour milk
	1 cup	1 tablespoon white vinegar or lemon juice stirred into 1 cup milk and allowed to stand 5 minutes
Cake flour	1 cup sifted	⅞ cup sifted all-purpose flour
Chocolate	1 square unsweetened	3 tablespoons unsweetened cocoa plus 1 tablespoon melted butter or shortening
Coconut	1½ cups fresh	1 cup dried shredded or 1⅓ cups dried flaked
	1 cup dried shredded	1⅓ cups dried flaked
Cornstarch	1 tablespoon	2 tablespoons flour
	1 tablespoon	4 teaspoons quick-cooking tapioca
Corn syrup	1 cup	1 cup granulated sugar plus ¼ cup liquid
Flour (all-purpose)	1 cup sifted	1 cup plus 2 tablespoons sifted cake flour
	1 tablespoon	1½ teaspoons cornstarch or 2 teaspoons quick-cooking tapioca
Ginger	½ teaspoon freshly grated	⅛–¼ teaspoon powdered ginger
Honey	1 cup	1¼ cups granulated sugar plus ¼ cup liquid
Lemon juice	1 teaspoon	½ teaspoon vinegar
	3 tablespoons fresh	2 tablespoons bottled
Lemon rind	1 teaspoon grated fresh	1 teaspoon dried
Milk (whole)	1 cup	¼ cup dry milk solids plus 1 cup water
	1 cup	½ cup evaporated milk plus ½ cup water
	1 cup	¼ cup nonfat dry milk solids plus 1 cup water plus 2½ teaspoons butter
Orange juice	⅓ cup fresh (juice of one orange)	¼ cup reconstituted frozen orange juice
Sour cream	1 cup	⅞ cup sour milk plus 3 tablespoons butter
Sugar (white granulated)	1 cup	1 cup superfine sugar
	1 cup	1 cup packed brown sugar
	1 cup	1¾ cup confectioners' sugar
	1 cup	½ cup maple syrup and ¼ cup corn syrup (reduce liquid in recipe by 2 tablespoons)
	1 cup	1 cup light molasses plus ¼ teaspoon baking soda (leave out baking powder)
Tapioca (quick cooking)	2 teaspoons	1 tablespoon flour or 1½ teaspoons cornstarch
Yogurt	1 cup	1 cup buttermilk
Yolks	2 yolks	1 whole egg

This scrumptious *Carrot Spice Cake* is topped with rosettes of *Cream Cheese Icing* and walnut halves. The sides are covered with chopped, toasted walnuts.

Cakes

C akes have a wonderful, long-
standing tradition, not only in
our culture but throughout the
world. Celebrations of all sorts,
from birthdays to weddings,
are not considered complete without
the cutting and sharing of a cake. But
cakes are not restricted to special
occasions. An ordinary day can become
memorable simply with the
sharing of a freshly baked cake.
Here we feature a multitude
of spectacular cakes, from the
traditional Chocolate Layer
Cake to the elegant
Greek Walnut Torte.

THE CAKE TRADITION

The close association of cake with special events has elevated this edible creation to a level all its own—a cake has become a universal symbol of a good, happy, and abundant life.

Cakes are enjoyed not only on special occasions; throughout the year we indulge in cakes. They are an important part of our everyday lives. Few activities in the kitchen are more challenging and enjoyable than preparing a cake from scratch. Sharing it later with friends and family is the ultimate reward.

This chapter presents an outstanding collection of recipes for cakes—from easy-to-make Chocolate-Almond Bundt Cake to a simply exquisite French Strawberry Mirror Cake. There are layer cakes, one-layer cakes, bundt and loaf cakes, and specialty cakes.

THE INGREDIENTS IN CAKE

Cake batters are usually made from flour, sugar, liquids, fat, and sometimes other ingredients. Butter cakes always contain butter or shortening and are leavened with baking powder or beaten eggs. Chiffon and angel cakes are made without butter and are leavened with eggs that are beaten separately. Tortes are light cakes in which ground nuts or bread crumbs replace all or part of the flour. Certain "quick" cakes are made from batters that contain oil instead of butter; the batter is simply stirred together and leavened with baking powder.

Cakes rise during baking because the combination of moisture in the batter and the distribution of tiny bubbles cause the batter to expand and rise in the presence of heat. The bubbles are created in two ways. A leavening agent such as baking powder will produce carbon dioxide bubbles in the presence of moisture. Other air bubbles are created by beating air into the ingredients, as when sugar and butter are creamed, when sugar and eggs are beaten

together (in sponge cake), or when egg whites are beaten separately and folded into the batter. It is essential to beat the cake batter as directed in the recipe in order to properly aerate the batter and produce a well-risen cake that will not collapse during or after baking (see "Beating Egg Whites and Folding," page 25).

The use of high-quality, fresh ingredients is one of the most important keys to creating a delicious cake. Follow the recommendations below concerning the use of various ingredients. Refer to the Flavor Pairings Chart on page 22 for a discussion of flavors and liqueurs most commonly used in cakes, and substitutions that can be made for them.

Flour Use cake flour when indicated for a lighter, more tender cake. Sift cake flour before measuring. If you wish to substitute all-purpose flour for cake flour in a recipe, subtract 2 tablespoons of flour for every cup of cake flour specified. Many all-purpose flours are presifted and do not need to be sifted before measuring.

Sugar Use white granulated sugar unless otherwise indicated.

Liquids Liquids used in cakes are eggs, water, milk, juice, sour cream, buttermilk, yogurt, cream, and others. Use eggs graded "large" unless otherwise directed. Separate eggs when cold. Use whole eggs, egg yolks, and egg whites at room temperature. Eggs may be measured by volume and weight. An egg is two-thirds white and one-third yolk.

Fat Use hydrogenated vegetable shortening or fresh unsalted butter. Lard should be avoided in cake making because it doesn't cream well. When oil is specified, use a light oil such as safflower oil.

ALL ABOUT CAKE PANS

Always use clean, dry, rust-free pans. Light- to medium-weight, shiny metal pans produce cakes with more tender, delicately browned crusts. Darker metal pans and glass pans produce darker brown, heavier (thicker) crusts. Reduce oven temperature by 25° F when using dark metal or glass pans. Refer to page 10 for complete information on pans and how to choose a substitute when you don't have the size called for in the recipe.

Preparing Cake Pans Spread an even layer of soft or melted shortening or butter evenly over the entire inside surface of the pan. Place a few tablespoons of flour in the pan; tilt pan in each direction until the entire buttered surface is dusted with a thin layer of flour. Invert the pan and tap it on a counter to remove excess flour. Using the bottom of the cake pan as a guide, trace around the pan onto a piece of parchment or waxed paper, cut it to fit, and place it on the bottom. Kitchen parchment is a coated paper used in baking. It is far less flammable than waxed paper and for that reason is preferable. When the cake is turned out after baking, it will not stick to the bottom of the pan.

Baking Cakes

The cake is done when it springs back when lightly touched in center with a fingertip and when it begins to pull away from the sides of the pan. Check the cake occasionally. A cake tester, toothpick, or wooden skewer should come out clean when inserted into the center of the cake.

Cool the cake as directed in the recipe. Cakes are often cooled in baking pans on wire cooling racks for 5 minutes before turning out. Run a knife around the cake to loosen it from the sides of pan, then invert the cake (turn it out) onto wire cooling racks. Cool completely at room temperature before icing or storing.

A pastry brush, a rubber spatula, a cooling rack, a wire whisk, cake pans, and measuring spoons are just a few of the utensils used in baking.

SUCCESSFUL CAKE BAKING

Success in baking depends upon a thorough reading of the entire recipe before you begin. Look up any terms or techniques you are unfamiliar with and make sure you have assembled all of the proper ingredients and recommended equipment. Carefully measure out the ingredients and have them at the specified temperature and in the condition indicated in the recipe. Think about how you would like to decorate the cake. Your chosen decoration might require extra icing or other ingredients. If you follow these guidelines but still experience difficulties, refer to the questions and answers below.

Why Does My Cake Fall in the Middle?

- ☐ Batter was overbeaten, creating excess aeration.
- ☐ Too much sugar was added to the batter.
- ☐ Too much baking powder was added.
- ☐ Too much liquid was added.
- ☐ Oven door was opened before cake was set or cake was disturbed by banging oven door.
- ☐ Cake was undercooked.

Why Does My Cake Rise to a Peak in the Center?

- ☐ A hard (high-gluten) flour was used instead of soft flour (cake flour).
- ☐ Batter was overbeaten after flour was added. (This overactivates the gluten in the flour, creating a tough cake.)
- ☐ Oven was too hot. Cake rose too quickly.

Why Is My Cake Tough, Flat, and Heavy?

- ☐ Batter was underbeaten, causing insufficient aeration.
- ☐ Not enough sugar was added.
- ☐ Not enough baking powder was added.

FREEZING CAKES AND ICINGS

See page 55 for the best way to wrap cakes for freezing. The times indicated below are for goods stored at 0° F.

Butter or Pound Cakes Unfrosted: Wrap, label, and date. Freeze for up to four months. To thaw: Loosen wrapping and thaw at room temperature.

Frosted: Chill frosted cakes on a tray in freezer (uncovered) until firm. Wrap, label, and date. Freeze for up to two months. To thaw: Remove wrapping and thaw at room temperature or in refrigerator.

Chiffon or Sponge Cakes Wrap, freeze, and thaw as for butter or pound cakes. Freeze unfrosted cakes up to six months. Freeze frosted cakes up to two months.

Spices Certain spices, such as nutmeg and cloves, intensify in flavor when they are frozen, so use slightly less than the amount called for in the recipe. Freeze and thaw as for butter cakes.

Cheesecakes Chill on a tray in freezer (uncovered) until firm. Wrap, label, and date. Freeze for up to four months. Thaw in wrapping in refrigerator.

Fruitcake Wrap, label, and date. Freeze for up to 12 months. Thaw in wrapping at room temperature.

Icings Butter-based icings can be frozen successfully for up to two months in rigid containers. Icings based on egg whites or whipped cream do not freeze well.

CAKE DECORATION AND PRESENTATION

How you decorate a cake and the shape you bake it in can set your cake apart from all the rest. Almost every recipe in this chapter contains detailed assembly and decoration instructions that will help you create a truly distinctive, stunning cake.

When cakes are baked to celebrate an occasion, you can tailor your decorations accordingly. It is sometimes handy to bake the cake in a shape that suits your event. Oblong cakes that can be iced and transported in their tins are perfect picnic fare. The same cake base could be baked in layers and elegantly adorned with buttercream rosettes or piped scrolls to serve at a dinner party. Cake decoration ranges from the way you texture an icing as you spread it on the cake to the application of decorations in intricate patterns on the cake.

Finishing the Cake

The outside of a cake can be covered with one of the following:

Confectioners' Sugar Finish the top of a cake quickly and simply by sifting a light layer of confectioners' sugar over the cake. Create a design with confectioners' sugar by laying a stencil, a fancy paper doily, a cutout snowflake, or strips of paper on top of the cake before sifting the confectioners' sugar over it. Carefully remove the stencil to reveal design. Powdered cocoa may also be sifted over a cake in this way. Use a combination of cocoa powder and confectioners' sugar to create a dark and light design.

Icing applied evenly in a smooth, flat layer is a common method of decorating a cake. Create a textured surface in icing with a flat metal spatula or knife (swirls, peaks, lines, etc.). Icing can also be applied in a smooth layer and textured with a comb scraper (serrated metal triangle) to create a grooved surface. There are many kinds of icings. Some must be spread on with a spatula or knife, and some can be piped on with a pastry bag and tip.

Glazes Cakes can be covered with a jelly glaze, a chocolate glaze, or a fondant icing glaze. A glaze is thinner than an icing. It is often poured over a cake rather than spread on.

Almond Paste Almond paste or marzipan can be rolled out and used to form the top layer or outside covering of a cake. Almond paste can also be molded or shaped to form cake decorations (roses, flowers, leaves, stems, animals, fruits, etc.). (See page 28 for a recipe for almond paste.)

Typical Cake Decorations

These are applied to the icing, glaze, or other surface covering of the cake to create patterns and add flavor.

Nuts Finely chopped, coarsely chopped, slivered, or sliced nuts, nut halves, or whole nuts can be used. Whole or halved nuts can be dipped in caramel or chocolate to decorate. Nuts taste and look best when lightly toasted in oven before they are used to decorate a cake.

Praline After a cake is iced, praline (powdered caramelized nuts) can be patted around the sides of the cake to add flavor, color, and texture to the icing (see page 24).

Fresh Fruit Either whole or sliced fresh fruit can be arranged decoratively on top of a cake. Fresh fruit is usually brushed with a thin jelly glaze to make it shine.

Cookie Crumbs Finely crushed cookies can be used in the same manner as praline to decorate a cake.

Chocolate Melted and tempered chocolate can be used in many ways to create cake decorations. Chocolate curls, rolls, and ruffles can be created from melted chocolate and transferred to the cake when set. For information about how to make these decorations, see pages 32–33.

You can also wrap the cake in a paper-thin chocolate ribbon (see page 33), or chocolate can be placed in a pastry bag and used to write directly on an iced or plain cake.

Miscellaneous Decorations Candied (glacé) orange, lemon, or citron peel (candied peel can be chopped or cut in julienne strips, or pieces of it can be dipped in melted chocolate); dried fruit (raisins, currants); crystallized violets, roses, or mimosa; candy coffee beans; silver balls; gold leaf; chocolate vermicelli; crystal sugar; preserved ginger; cloth or paper ribbon can be tied around cake after icing is firm; fresh flowers or leaves (leaves and flowers should be free from any harmful spray).

Sauces Cakes can be served with a sauce on the side. Chocolate sauce, fruit sauce (i.e., raspberry, strawberry, melba), and vanilla custard sauce (*crème anglaise*) are all good possibilities.

Cutting and Trimming Cake In addition to applying decorations to a cake, you can cut or trim a cake to enhance its decoration. See, for example, the White and Dark Chocolate Hazelnut Cake (page 48) or Heart-Shaped Strawberry Sponge Cake (page 30). A thin piece is trimmed off each end of the White and Dark Chocolate Hazelnut Cake to expose its alternating layers of dark and white chocolate. The edges of the Heart-Shaped Strawberry Sponge Cake are trimmed to halve the whole strawberries at the edge of the cake, creating an attractive design. Use your imagination to apply such techniques to other cakes.

Tools Useful in Cake Decorating Artist's paintbrushes; pastry brushes; flexible, narrow stainless steel spatulas in various sizes (bent and straight); toothpicks; skewers; cake-decorating needles to trace out design on cake; metal leaf mold (for almond-paste leaves); sets of cutters in various shapes and sizes; comb scraper (metal triangle with serrated edges); revolving cake decorating stand.

The Cake Plate The plate the cake is presented on can dramatically enhance its presentation. Choose a plate or platter that contributes to the overall effect you are trying to create with your cake.

Serving Finally, the way you slice the cake and place it on each plate is very important. Use a sharp knife (in some cases a serrated knife works best) to slice the cake. Clean the knife after each cut to remove accumulated icing. A cake slice can be presented lying down on its side or standing up (when possible or when more attractive). Try to include part of the top decoration in each serving.

CAKE-DECORATING TECHNIQUES

Decorating cakes makes them extra special. Like calligraphy, drawing, or playing the piano, cake decorating takes practice. The following photographs demonstrate a variety of different designs created using a pastry bag with only two different tips. A paper piping cone was used to do writing and line work. The paper piping cone designs can also be piped out on parchment paper, chilled, and transferred to pastries when they are firm.

The decorations were piped onto a marble surface rather than a cake to show clearly the variations that can be pressed from the same tip, simply by adjusting the way you manipulate the bag.

It is important not to overfill the pastry bag or piping cone, so that you can control the bag. Press with even pressure. Use the other hand merely to guide the bag. It is very important to hold the tip away from the surface of the cake—a half inch at least—so that the design can take shape without being squashed or destroyed. This is a mistake most beginners make.

Practice these designs on a piece of waxed paper or other clean surface. Repetition will lead to perfection. And before you decorate directly on a cake, warm up by practicing on a clean surface. If you happen to make a mistake on the cake, scrape it off with a spatula and start over. Rechill the icing if it warms up too much.

1. *A few basic tools make cake decorating easy. Left to right: A revolving cake-decorating stand holds ornamenting tubes, a canvas pastry bag, and a two-part coupling unit. On the marble below are small and large offset flexible metal spatulas for icing cakes. Serrated triangular comb scrapers create texture in icing.*

2. *Place the coupler in the pastry bag so it projects slightly from the hole at the bottom of the bag. Twist the pastry bag just above the tip and push the twisted portion of the bag into the tip. This blocks the opening and prevents the filling from running out of the bag while you are filling it. Hold bag cuffed over left hand; fill bag no more than half full. Then unfold cuff and press sides of bag together at the top and run your fingers down the outside of the bag toward the filling to force the filling into the lower half of the bag.*

3. *To pipe decorations: Once the bag is filled, untwist the small end of the bag; hold the top of the bag between your right thumb and index finger just above the filling. Squeeze the filling out of the bag with the remaining fingers of your right hand. Use your other hand as a guide while piping decorations. Periodically twist the bag to increase pressure on the filling and keep it moving out of the tip. (If you are left-handed reverse these directions.) Lines 1 through 5 were piped out with a small open-star ornamenting tube. Line 6 employed a leaf ornamenting tube.*

Line 1 is a chain of stars. Line 2 is a chain of rosettes. Line 3 is a chain of shells. Line 4 is an S-curve in a serpentine ribbon. Line 5 is a fleur-de-lis. Line 6 features a chain of leaves (ruffle).

4. *Fill a paper piping cone no more than half full with melted chocolate (see illustrations on opposite page). Hold bag in right hand and gently press to force chocolate out of bag. Hold tip of bag at least ¼ inch away from surface of cake; use left hand to guide bag only.*

Lines 1 through 4 are typical border designs. Line 5 shows how to write on cakes with chocolate. Line 6 is a classic design.

How to Use a Pastry Bag, Coupling Unit, and Ornamenting Tubes

Pastry bags are available in nylon, cloth, and plastic, in a variety of sizes. Nylon pastry bags made in France or plastic pastry bags without reinforced tips are best. Pastry bags can also be made quite easily and inexpensively from parchment paper in a variety of sizes (these are called paper piping cones). Disposable pastry bags are convenient when you are using several different colors of icing to decorate a cake.

The Coupling Unit The coupling unit consists of two plastic pieces: a coupler and a coupling screw. This unit allows you to change ornamenting tubes on the end of your pastry bag without switching to a new bag. Ornamenting tubes are made of tinned metal and come in a variety of different sizes with openings of different shapes. The tubes have a number stamped on one side to identify the size of the tube. Tubes are usually referred to by their number rather than by the size of their opening.

How to Assemble Bag and Tips Place the coupler in the pastry bag so it projects slightly from the hole at the bottom of the bag. Sometimes it is necessary to trim a piece off the small end of the pastry bag (with scissors) to enlarge the opening to accommodate the coupler. Place the desired ornamenting tube over the coupler projecting from the end of the bag. Fit the coupling screw over the tube and screw it on so that it catches part of the bag and holds the tip in place.

The following tubes are the ones most often needed to decorate cakes or pipe out meringues, cream puff paste, or ladyfingers. Plain tubes are best for writing on cakes and for making lines, stems, dots, or line drawings. Open-star tubes are best for small or large rosettes, stars, and border designs. Closed-star tubes are best for rosettes and flowers. Leaf tubes are used for leaves. Other tubes are useful if you want to decorate cakes elaborately.

Buttercream Icing (page 23) and Chantilly Cream (page 59) are suitable for piping. Any icing that is thick enough to hold its form when pressed through a tube and is soft enough to flow smoothly out of the bag can be used to decorate a cake. Plain, melted semisweet chocolate (cooled to 86° F) can be used to pipe line decorations (see pages 32–33). Use a small pastry bag fitted with a narrow writing tube or a paper piping cone with a tiny opening to pipe thin lines.

Cleaning and Storing Pastry Bags and Tips Wash disassembled coupling unit, ornamenting tube, and pastry bag in hot, sudsy water; rinse well. It is best to drape the bag over something that will hold it open while it dries completely. If bags are folded up and put away when still wet, they have a tendency to mildew and develop a sour smell. Keep pastry bags for savory fillings separate from those used to pipe sweet icings; pastry bags sometimes retain the odor of a strong filling. Dry ornamenting tubes immediately and store in a dry place. They will rust if left to air dry or if stored while wet.

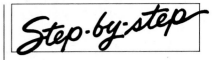

HOW TO MAKE A PAPER PIPING CONE

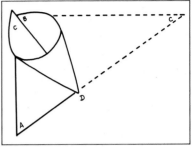

Cut a square of parchment paper in half to form two triangles. (Use only one of the triangles.) Precut parchment triangles are also available in cookware stores. Take the right-hand point (C) on the longest side of the triangle and fold it in toward the middle point (B) at the top. Then take the opposite point (A) and fold it around until it also meets the middle point (B) at the top. The three points meet to form a closed-tip (D) paper cone.

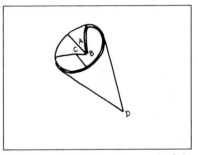

Fold the point at the open end of the cone over toward the closed tip of the cone to prevent the cone from unraveling.

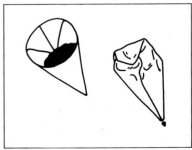

To use the cone, fill it no more than half full. Fold the open end of the piping cone down toward the filling. Cut the closed end of the cone with scissors to form a plain tube opening of the size needed.

FLAVOR PAIRINGS CHART

Cakes and pastries usually have one or two ingredients that dominate the overall taste. These ingredients can be complemented or enhanced by the addition of other flavorings. If you are making substitutions (apples instead of pears, for instance) or creating a new recipe, this chart will help you choose compatible flavors.

You will notice that fresh fruit is most often paired with a fruit liqueur or brandy, citrus rind, juice, or extract, or almond or vanilla extract. Coffee is paired with rum, brandy, or coffee liqueur. Find the dominant ingredient in your pastry on the left and pair it with one of the flavor suggestions on the right.

Dominant Taste	Suggested Flavorings
Almonds	Amaretto, almond extract, kirsch and other fruit liqueurs, rum, brandy, orange rind
Apples	Apple brandy, rum, Cognac, lemon rind
Apricots	Apricot brandy, kirsch, almond extract
Bananas	Rum, vanilla extract
Berries	Berry brandies or liqueurs, kirsch, citrus rind or juice
Chestnuts	Rum
Chocolate	Liqueurs: orange, coffee, mint, nut, fruit brandies: grape (Cognac) or fruit rum, bourbon, whiskey extracts: vanilla, almond, coffee, mint also: orange rind, nuts, berries, praline
Coffee	Coffee liqueur, rum, brandy
Cranberries	Orange-flavored liqueur, orange or lemon rind or juice, walnuts
Figs	Kirsch, raspberry liqueur, orange rind, raspberries
Grapes	Cognac
Grapefruit	Citrus rind or juice, rum
Hazelnuts	Hazelnut liqueur, rum, fruit brandies (to complement any fruit in cake)
Lemons	Citrus rind or juice, rum, lemon extract
Limes	Citrus rind or juice, rum
Mangoes	Rum, lime juice

Dominant Taste	Suggested Flavorings
Melons	Lime juice, lemon juice, fresh mint
Mocha	Coffee liqueur, rum, brandy, mint, chocolate liqueur
Nectarines	Kirsch, orange-flavored liqueur, orange juice or rind
Oranges	Orange-flavored liqueur, orange or lemon rind or juice, rum
Papayas	Lemon or lime rind or juice
Peaches	Almonds, almond extract, amaretto, kirsch, orange rind or juice, fresh mint
Pears	Pear-flavored brandy, Marsala, almonds or almond extract
Pecans	Rum, bourbon, Cognac, orange-flavored liqueur, orange rind or juice
Persimmons	Orange-flavored liqueur, orange rind or juice, vanilla extract
Pineapple	Kirsch, rum
Pine nuts	Rum, orange-flavored liqueur, citrus rind or juice
Plums	Plum-flavored brandy
Pumpkin	Cognac or apple brandy, rum, bourbon
Rhubarb	Strawberry brandy, kirsch, orange juice
Tangerines	Citrus rind or juice, tangerine brandy, rum
Walnuts	Rum, lemon rind, orange rind, coffee, chocolate

BUTTERCREAM ICING

This creamy, versatile icing is used, in varying amounts, in many of the cake recipes included in this chapter. It can be flavored in a multitude of ways to go well with many types of cakes. It works very well for decorating with a pastry bag.

For 1 cup

2 egg yolks
⅓ cup sugar
¼ cup water
½ cup unsalted butter, softened

For 1½ cups

3 egg yolks
½ cup sugar (scant; 7 tbsp)
⅓ cup water
¾ cup unsalted butter, softened

For 2 cups

4 egg yolks
½ cup sugar
⅓ cup water
1 cup unsalted butter, softened

For 3 cups

6 egg yolks
1 cup sugar (scant; 14 tbsp)
½ cup water
1½ cups unsalted butter, softened

1. Beat yolks in a medium stainless bowl until light.

2. Combine sugar and water in a heavy 2½-quart saucepan; stir over medium heat until sugar dissolves and syrup comes to a boil. As sugar is dissolving, wash down any sugar crystals that cling to the sides of the pan with a pastry brush dipped in cold water.

3. Boil syrup gently, without stirring, until it reaches 239° F (soft-ball stage; see page 24). When syrup reaches the soft-ball stage, immediately remove from heat and pour into the yolks, beating constantly as you pour. Continue to beat until the mixture is light, fluffy, and cool to the touch.

TO FLAVOR BUTTERCREAM ICING

Type of Buttercream	Flavoring	Amount of Buttercream			
		1 cup	1½ cups	2 cups	3 cups
Chocolate	semisweet chocolate (melted and cooled)	3 oz	4 oz	6 oz	8 oz
Citrus fruit	finely grated orange or lemon rind	1 tsp	1½ tsp	2 tsp	3 tsp
Coffee	coffee extract or instant coffee dissolved in boiling water	to taste 2 tsp 1 tbsp	1 tbsp 1 tbsp	4 tsp 1½ tbsp	1½ tbsp 2 tbsp
Fruit	fruit purée and/or fruit liqueur	⅓ cup	½ cup	⅔ cup	1 cup
		to taste; see Liqueur below			
Liqueur	liqueur or brandy	2 tsp	1 tbsp	1½ tbsp	2 tbsp
Mocha	semisweet chocolate (melted and cooled) and coffee extract	3 oz	4 oz	6 oz	8 oz
		flavor with coffee extract to taste or with instant coffee in amounts under Coffee			
Nuts	finely ground toasted nuts	3 tbsp	⅓ cup	½ cup	¾ cup
Praline	finely ground caramelized nuts	2 tbsp	¼ cup	⅓ cup	½ cup
Vanilla	vanilla extract	1 tsp	1½ tsp	2 tsp	1 tbsp
White chocolate	white chocolate (melted and cooled)	3 oz	4 oz	6 oz	8 oz

4. In medium bowl of electric mixer, cream butter. Gradually beat butter into yolk mixture, 2 tablespoons at a time, until smooth, shiny, and spreadable. At this point you may fold in some stiffly whipped cream or vanilla pastry cream to lighten the buttercream (this is optional). Flavor the buttercream according to the chart above. Use buttercream immediately or refrigerate until ready to use. Store up to 3 days in the refrigerator or freeze up to 2 months.

To use cold buttercream, remove from refrigerator, allow to warm to room temperature (20 to 30 minutes), then beat icing until smooth, shiny, and spreadable.

Note If the buttercream separates at any point after the butter is added, the butter may be too cold. Wrap a hot, wet towel around the bowl; then beat until smooth. If you think the buttercream has warmed up too much, refrigerate a few minutes, then beat until smooth.

PRALINE

Praline consists of ground caramelized nuts. It is used to decorate cakes and is added to fillings and even cake batters.

  ½ cup whole hazelnuts, skinned (see page 67)
  ½ cup whole natural almonds (with skins)
  ¾ cup sugar
  ¼ cup water

1. Heat nuts in a 350° F oven for a few minutes. Place sugar and the water in a heavy 2½-quart saucepan. Bring to a boil to dissolve sugar.

2. Cook sugar syrup over medium-high heat, without stirring, until syrup reaches 248° F on candy thermometer (hard-ball stage; see "Sugar Syrup Stages," at right). Remove from heat and stir in warm nuts. Stir until mixture resembles nuts in white sand.

3. Return pot to stove and cook over medium heat, stirring constantly, until the sugar liquefies and turns a rich brown caramel color. Pour onto an oiled baking sheet. Cool completely.

4. Break praline into small pieces and grind in small jar of electric blender or in food processor. Grind with short bursts until it is the desired texture. Praline is usually added to creams and icings in the form of a fine powder. More coarsely ground praline is used to decorate the outside of a cake or to add a crunchy texture. Store in an airtight container in a cool room up to 3 weeks or in freezer for up to 3 months.

Makes 2 cups finely ground praline powder.

COOKING SUGAR SYRUP

Some of the preparations in this chapter, such as Buttercream Icing and Praline, require the addition of sugar syrup that is cooked to a specific sugar concentration. The concentration of sugar in a sugar syrup can be measured by its temperature reading on a candy thermometer or by its appearance when dropped into ice water. For the inexperienced, a candy-thermometer reading is the most reliable way to measure the sugar concentration.

It is important to follow the steps below when making a sugar syrup and when cooking the syrup to a specified stage (temperature). Before testing, remove the pan from the heat so that the sugar syrup does not continue to cook.

1. Check the accuracy of your candy thermometer by placing it in water and bringing the water to a boil. The thermometer should register 212° F at boiling point.

2. Before using, warm the candy thermometer by placing it in a glass of hot tap water.

3. Place sugar in a heavy-bottomed pan with smooth sides or an unlined copper pan. Add enough water to dissolve sugar (about ⅓ cup water will dissolve 1 cup sugar).

4. Place over low heat and stir just until sugar dissolves. Brush sides of pan with a pastry brush dipped in water to wash down any sugar crystals that cling to the sides of the pan. It is very important to dissolve the sugar before the syrup comes to a boil.

5. Once the syrup comes to a boil, allow it to boil undisturbed (do not stir again or the syrup will crystalize). Place the candy thermometer in the pan and allow the syrup to boil gently until it reaches the required temperature. Use the syrup at once. You can prevent the syrup from reaching a higher temperature by placing the pan in a bowl of ice water momentarily. This arrests cooking and keeps the syrup at desired temperature longer.

6. *To test syrup without a candy thermometer:* Remove a few drops of syrup from the pan with a spoon; dip spoon in ice water; gather syrup in fingertips and try to roll it into a ball. The sugar will exhibit characteristics of one of the stages discussed below.

Sugar Syrup Stages

Thread Stage (217° F to 223° F on candy thermometer) Syrup forms thin threads when a spoon is dipped in syrup and then some of the syrup on the spoon is dropped into ice water. It cannot be gathered into a ball.

Soft-Ball Stage (238° F to 240° F) Syrup will form a soft, pliable ball when rolled between fingers in ice water.

Hard-Ball Stage (248° F) Syrup will form a firm, pliable ball when rolled between fingers in ice water. The ball is well formed and offers some resistance when pressed.

Soft-Crack Stage (264° F to 270° F) Syrup can be stretched into firm but still-elastic strands in ice water.

Hard-Crack Stage (293° F to 295° F) Syrup will solidify when dropped into ice water and can be snapped in half easily.

Light Caramel Stage (320° F to 338° F) Syrup is a light amber color (light golden brown) when poured onto a white plate.

Dark Caramel Stage (350° F) Caramel is a dark red-brown color. If caramel is cooked beyond this stage, it burns and becomes very bitter.

ROYAL ICING

This icing is used in a decorative manner on cakes that have already been iced with buttercream or another surface icing. For birthday cakes and other special occasion cakes, it allows you to add the professional touch of special inscriptions and designs. It's easy to make and fun to use. Spoon some into a small pastry bag fitted with a writing tube, or make a fine-tipped paper piping cone (see page 21). Practice your decorations on waxed paper before putting them on the cake. Make a pencil sketch on the waxed paper and then trace over it with icing using the paper piping cone. This icing can be tinted in a variety of colors with food coloring, so mix and match. Royal Icing should be stiff enough to hold its shape when piped out, but it must also be pliable enough to flow through the ornamenting tube or piping cone. This icing firms up and hardens when dry.

> 1¼ cups sifted confectioners'
> sugar
> 1 egg white
> 1 teaspoon strained lemon juice

1. Beat ¾ cup of the sugar with egg white and lemon juice until thick and white (approximately 10 minutes). Add the remaining ½ cup sugar and beat until stiff. Icing may be tinted with food coloring.

2. To store icing for up to a week, lay a piece of plastic wrap directly on surface of icing; refrigerate.

Makes ¾ cup.

BEATING EGG WHITES AND FOLDING

When beating egg whites it is important to incorporate as much air into the whites as possible and create beaten whites with a stable, elastic foam. The elasticity of the egg white cells and the air enclosed in them allow the egg whites to expand during baking to form a light, well-risen cake. Overbeaten egg whites are less elastic and cannot stretch during baking without breaking and collapsing. Egg whites tend to deflate and separate if they are beaten ahead of time and left to stand for more than a minute or two. For maximum leavening power, beat egg whites just before you are ready to fold them into the batter.

☐ Separate egg whites from egg yolks when eggs are cold. Carefully avoid getting any of the yolks in the whites. The egg whites will not mount properly if there is any trace of yolk or other fat in the whites.

☐ Have egg whites at room temperature. Have bowl and whisk or whip attachment of electric mixer very clean and free from grease. Egg whites should be beaten in a large, unlined bowl. Beat egg whites by hand with a balloon whisk or by machine with the whip attachment of an electric mixer. If regular beaters are used, the beaten whites will develop less volume. The resulting cake will be heavier and flatter.

☐ Beat whites at medium speed until foamy. When not using a copper bowl, add ¼ teaspoon cream of tartar (for every 6 whites); gradually increase speed and continue to beat until whites hold soft, stiff peaks when whisk is lifted from bowl. Gradually add sugar (1 to 2 tablespoons at a time) and continue beating until whites hold stiff, glossy peaks. Do not overbeat whites or they will separate and form lumps when you try to incorporate them into a batter.

☐ Some recipes direct you to stir some of the whites into the batter. This lightens the batter so the remaining whites can be folded into the batter without deflating them.

Folding is a method of manually incorporating one mixture (or ingredient) into another without deflating the air in the lighter mixture. Folding beaten egg whites into a batter can have two functions: (1) to lighten the texture of a batter or cream; (2) to act as a leavening agent in batters that are to be baked.

Folding is accomplished with the hand itself or with a flat spoon or spatula. Place the mixture that is to be "folded in" on top of the other mixture. Cut down through the center of both mixtures with one sharp motion, scrape across the bottom of the bowl and up one side of the bowl with a lifting motion (as you give the bowl a quarter turn with the other hand). This movement brings the mixture up from below and lightly envelops the mixture being folded in. Repeat the process until the two mixtures are just combined into one homogeneous mixture. Work quickly but lightly, taking care not to deflate the lighter mixture.

FOMBONNE'S CHOCOLATE CAKE

After baking, this rich one-layer chocolate cake is split into three layers and iced with Chocolate Sour Cream Icing. Toasted hazelnuts add flavor and crunch to the top.

- 5 egg yolks
- 2 cups sifted confectioners' sugar
- 10 ounces semisweet chocolate, melted and cooled
- 9 tablespoons unsalted butter, melted and cooled
- 1 cup sifted cake flour
- ⅔ cup sifted cornstarch
- 2 teaspoons baking powder
- 5 egg whites
- ½ cup toasted, finely chopped hazelnuts
- 10 whole hazelnuts

Chocolate Sour Cream Icing

- 9 ounces semisweet chocolate
- 1 cup sour cream

1. Preheat oven to 350° F. Butter and flour an 8- by 2-inch round cake pan (see Pan Substitution chart, page 10, if you do not have this size pan); line bottom with waxed paper.

2. Place egg yolks in large bowl of electric mixer. Gradually add 1⅔ cup of the sugar to yolks and beat until light and fluffy. Stir chocolate and butter together and add to yolk mixture; beat until smooth.

3. Sift flour, cornstarch, and baking powder together. Stir into batter (batter will be very stiff).

4. Beat egg whites until they hold soft peaks; add remaining sugar and beat until stiff but still glossy. Stir one third of whites into batter to lighten it. Gently fold in remaining whites.

5. Pour batter into cake pan and bake until done (40 to 50 minutes). Cool in pan 10 minutes, then turn out onto wire rack to finish cooling. Use a long, serrated knife to split the cake horizontally into 3 equal layers. Ice the cake with Chocolate Sour Cream Icing and allow icing to set before decorating further.

6. *To decorate cake:* Cut out five ¾-inch-wide strips of waxed paper and lay them about ¾ inch apart on top of the cake. Sprinkle chopped toasted hazelnuts on cake not covered by paper strips. Carefully remove strips. Place whole hazelnuts on top of cake, around its perimeter.

Serves 10.

Chocolate Sour Cream Icing

Melt chocolate; cool. Gradually stir in sour cream. Ice cake immediately.

ZESTY LEMON-FILLED CAKE

Nothing is more refreshing than lemon. Three layers of zesty lemon curd fill this four-layer white cake.

- 9 tablespoons unsalted butter, softened
- ⅔ cup granulated sugar
- 2⅔ cups flour
- 1½ teaspoons baking powder
- ¾ cup milk
- 5 egg whites
- 2 tablespoons granulated sugar Confectioners' sugar

Lemon Filling

- 3 eggs
- 3 egg yolks
- 1 cup granulated sugar
- ⅔ cup lemon juice
- 2 teaspoons finely grated lemon rind
- ½ cup unsalted butter, softened

1. Preheat oven to 350° F. Butter and flour two 8- by 2-inch round cake pans; line bottom of each with a circle of waxed paper.

2. In large bowl of electric mixer, cream butter and the ⅔ cup granulated sugar together; beat until light.

3. Sift flour and baking powder together. Add to creamed mixture alternately with milk, beating well after each addition.

4. Beat egg whites until they hold soft peaks. Beat in the 2 tablespoons granulated sugar and beat until whites hold stiff peaks but are still glossy (do not overbeat). Stir one fourth of the whites into the batter to lighten it. Then gently fold in the remaining whites.

5. Divide the batter evenly between the 2 cake pans. Bake until cake tests done, about 40 minutes. Cool in pans 5 minutes, then turn out on wire racks to finish cooling. Prepare Lemon Filling and cool completely. Split each layer in half horizontally. Spread 3 of the layers with Lemon Filling and place layers one on top of another on a cake plate. Place fourth layer on top. Dust with confectioners' sugar.

Serves 8 to 10.

Lemon Filling Combine eggs, egg yolks, sugar, lemon juice, and grated lemon rind in a medium stainless steel bowl. Place over a pot of boiling water (double boiler fashion) and whisk over medium heat until the mixture thickens to the consistency of mayonnaise (5 minutes). Do not boil or mixture will curdle. Remove from heat and whisk in butter, 2 tablespoons at a time. Cool to room temperature. Chill in refrigerator until ready to fill cake.

CHOCOLATE LAYER CAKE

To enjoy the best of two worlds, combine traditional American dark chocolate cake with a French chocolate buttercream. This moist layer cake would be equally delicious with vanilla, coffee, mocha, or praline buttercream. Split the layers to create a four-layer extravaganza.

 ¾ cup unsweetened cocoa
   powder
 ¾ cup boiling water
 ½ cup vegetable shortening
   or butter
 2 cups sugar
 2 eggs
 1 teaspoon vanilla extract
 ¼ teaspoon salt
 1½ teaspoons baking soda
 1 cup buttermilk
 2 cups sifted cake flour
 2 cups Chocolate Buttercream
   Icing (see page 23)

1. Preheat oven to 350° F. Butter and lightly flour two 8- by 2-inch round cake pans; line bottom of each with a circle of waxed paper.

2. Stir cocoa into boiling water until smooth; set aside.

3. In large bowl of electric mixer, Cream shortening and sugar together until light and fluffy. Add eggs, one at a time, beating after each addition. Beat in vanilla and salt.

4. Stir baking soda into buttermilk. Add ½ cup of the flour to egg mixture; then add ⅓ cup buttermilk mixture. Continue to add flour and buttermilk alternately, beating well after each addition. Stir in cocoa mixture.

5. Divide the batter evenly between the two cake pans. Bake until done (30 to 35 minutes). Cool in pans 5 minutes, then turn out on wire racks to finish cooling. Ice and decorate with Chocolate Buttercream Icing.

Serves 8 to 10.

Variation For a four-layer cake, slice each layer horizontally into two thin layers, with a long, serrated knife. Place layers one on top of another with buttercream between the layers.

This slice of luscious Chocolate Layer Cake with Chocolate Buttercream Icing is an irresistible temptation.

ALMOND PASTE AND MARZIPAN

Both almond paste and marzipan can be purchased in the specialty food section of grocery stores or in gourmet food shops. Try different brands to discover the ones whose taste and texture you like most.

Both should be smooth and pliable for ease in rolling out and modeling. To roll out either almond paste or marzipan, dust work surface lightly with confectioners' sugar and roll out with rolling pin. Tint almond paste or marzipan by kneading a few drops of food coloring into the paste. Pale tints are usually the most appetizing on pastry. Almond paste or marzipan can be modeled to form flowers, stems, leaves, and other decorative shapes. To make your own almond paste or marzipan, see recipes below.

In the photo above, green-tinted marzipan was rolled out and then applied to a leaf mold. The marzipan takes the shape of a leaf even with the detailing of the veins. After removal from the mold it can be placed on a cake for decoration.

HOMEMADE ALMOND PASTE

> 2 cups powdered (very finely ground) blanched almonds
> 2¼ cups sifted confectioners' sugar
> 1 to 2 egg whites, beaten until foamy

Combine almonds and sugar in a bowl. Stir well to blend. Gradually stir in enough egg whites to moisten almond mixture. Gather mixture into a ball; knead until smooth. Wrap well and refrigerate. Keeps for 1 week.

To make almond paste more pliable and easier to roll out, work a little fondant into it. Fondant is a sticky white icing available at bakeries or stores that sell cake-decorating supplies. To roll out almond paste, dust work surface with confectioners' sugar.

Makes about 1 pound.

HOMEMADE MARZIPAN

Marzipan is similar to almond paste, but is more pliable and sweeter.

> 2 cups sugar
> ¾ cup water
> 3½ cups powdered (finely ground) blanched almonds
> 2 egg whites, beaten until foamy

1. Combine sugar and water in saucepan. Cook to 240° F (soft-ball stage; see page 25). Remove from heat; stir until cloudy. Then stir in almonds.

2. Stir in egg whites and cook over low heat until mixture firms slightly. Dust work surface with confectioners' sugar. Knead marzipan until pliable. Wrap well and store in refrigerator for up to 1 month.

Makes 1¾ pounds.

POPPY SEED CAKE WITH CREAM CHEESE FROSTING

A moist poppy seed layer cake is delicious with a cream cheese frosting. This recipe has just the right amount of poppy seed.

> ⅔ cup milk
> ⅓ cup poppy seed
> 2¼ cups sifted cake flour
> 1 tablespoon baking powder
> ¼ teaspoon salt
> 1¼ cups sugar
> ½ cup butter, softened
> 2 teaspoons vanilla extract
> ½ cup milk
> 3 large egg whites
> ¼ cup sugar
> 2 tablespoons poppy seed, for decoration

Cream Cheese Frosting

> 6 ounces cream cheese, softened
> ¼ cup unsalted butter, softened
> 2 cups sifted confectioners' sugar
> 1 teaspoon lemon juice

1. Preheat oven to 350° F. Butter and flour two 8- by 2-inch round cake pans; line bottom of each with a circle of waxed paper.

2. Bring the ⅔ cup milk to a boil; remove from heat and stir in poppy seed; cool to room temperature.

3. Sift together flour, baking powder, and salt; set aside.

4. In large electric mixer bowl, cream the 1¼ cups sugar and butter together; beat until light. Add vanilla.

5. Combine poppy seed mixture and the ½ cup milk. Add this mixture alternately with flour to the creamed mixture, adding one third of each mixture at a time.

6. Beat egg whites until they hold soft peaks. Add the ¼ cup sugar, a little at a time, and beat until whites hold stiff, glossy peaks (do not overbeat). Gently fold into batter. Divide batter evenly between the 2 cake pans. Bake until done (30 minutes) or until the cake draws away from side of pan or cake tester comes out clean. Cool in pans 10 minutes, then turn out onto wire racks to finish cooling.

7. Frost with Cream Cheese Frosting. Decorate with poppy seed.

Serves 10 to 12.

Cream Cheese Frosting Cream together cream cheese and butter. Add confectioners' sugar and lemon juice; beat until creamy. If frosting is too runny, add more sugar. If it is too stiff, add a little milk.

This moist, two-layer Poppy Seed Cake is decorated with Cream Cheese Frosting and poppy seed. The striped effect is achieved by placing strips of paper over the top of the cake, then sprinkling the poppy seed onto the icing. A variety of designs can be made by using different templates.

HEART-SHAPED STRAWBERRY SPONGE CAKE

This special-occasion cake is perfect for Valentine's Day, but it wins hearts the year around. For variety you can make it with kiwis or poached pears or peaches instead of strawberries. It can be baked in many different shapes. If you tire of hearts, make it round, square, or oblong.

    4   eggs
    ⅔   cup sugar
    ½   teaspoon vanilla extract
    ¾   cup sifted cake flour
    3   tablespoons unsalted butter,
        melted and cooled
   30   medium strawberries
    ⅓   cup water
    ¼   cup sugar
    2   tablespoons kirsch
    3   cups Buttercream Icing
        (see page 23)

Almond-Paste Decorations

    7   to 10 ounces almond paste
        or marzipan (see page 28)
        Red or green food coloring
        (optional)
        Sifted confectioners' sugar

1. Preheat oven to 350° F. Butter and lightly flour a 6-cup heart-shaped pan (8 inches wide by 2 inches deep or 9 inches wide by 1½ inches deep). Line bottom with waxed paper.

2. Place eggs and the ⅔ cup sugar in a 4-quart stainless steel mixing bowl over a pot of boiling water and whisk until mixture is lukewarm (105° F). Immediately remove from heat, add vanilla, and whisk (or beat with electric mixer) until the batter reaches the ribbon stage (see page 24). Sift the flour over the batter, one third at a time, folding in each third with a rubber spatula as lightly as possible. Stir ½ cup of the batter into the melted butter to lighten it. Fold butter mixture quickly and gently into batter.

3. Pour batter into prepared pan and bake until cake shrinks slightly from the sides of the pan and top springs back when lightly touched (25 to 30 minutes). Cool in pan 5 minutes, then turn out onto wire rack to finish cooling.

4. Prepare Buttercream Icing and Almond-Paste Decorations.

5. Hull the strawberries and trim their bases so they are all the same height. Wash and drain well.

6. *To assemble cake:* Cut a cardboard heart ½ inch smaller than your heart-shaped cake and cover it with aluminum foil. Place the heart-shaped sponge cake on the cardboard. Split the cake horizontally into 2 equal layers with a long, serrated knife. Remove the top layer.

7. In a small saucepan, heat the water and sugar, stirring until sugar dissolves and syrup comes to a boil. Remove from heat, cool to room temperature. Stir in kirsch. Brush the bottom cake layer lightly with this kirsch syrup. Spread about ¼ inch of buttercream over this layer. Stand the strawberries on their wide ends very close together all over the bottom layer. Place a line of berries along the outer edges of the heart so the berries extend about ⅛ inch over the edge. Place all but ¼ cup of the buttercream in a pastry bag fitted with a tube tip and pipe buttercream down into the crevices around the berries and all over them. Make sure all the spaces are filled. Then smooth the buttercream over the berries with a narrow metal spatula.

8. Place the other layer of sponge cake on top and brush it with the remaining kirsch syrup until just moist but not soggy. You may have some syrup left over. Spread the remaining ¼ cup of buttercream over the top. Place the almond-paste heart on top and press lightly to adhere. Refrigerate for at least one hour or until the buttercream is firm. When the cake is cold, trim the outer edges all around with a very sharp, thin knife. Try to cut through the outer line of strawberries to halve them vertically. This will expose a pattern of halved strawberries all around the cake.

9. There are several ways to decorate the top. You can glaze some strawberries with warm currant jelly and set them on top surrounded by a few green almond-paste leaves. You can also write on or decorate the top with Buttercream or Royal Icing. If you are feeling artistic you can fashion a pink almond-paste rose and green leaves for a decoration.

10. Remove cake from refrigerator and allow to warm up slightly before serving.

Serves 10 to 12.

Almond-Paste Decorations

1. Place 6 ounces of the almond paste in a bowl. Put a few drops of food coloring (if used) on the almond paste. Work the food coloring into the almond paste with your fingertips or with the paddle attachment of your electric mixer. Add the food coloring one drop at a time, and work in evenly. Omit food coloring if a natural tan color is desired.

2. *To roll out the almond paste:* Dust the work surface with sifted confectioners' sugar. Roll the paste into a sheet that is ⅛ inch thick and 8½ inches in diameter. If the dough breaks when you are working with it, roll it up into a ball and start over. Dust the surface with confectioners' sugar frequently to avoid sticking. When the paste is rolled out, place the heart-shaped baking tin on top of it and cut around it with a sharp knife. Place the almond-paste heart on a waxed paper-lined baking sheet and refrigerate until ready to place on top of the cake. Roll the trimmings into a ball and use to form leaves and/or flowers.

GREEK WALNUT TORTE

Since egg whites are the only leavening agent in this torte, it is important to beat them properly and to fold them into the batter without deflating them. Use purchased candied orange rind if you prefer.

    1 pound shelled walnuts
    6 tablespoons dry bread crumbs
    9 egg yolks
    ¾ cup sugar
    2 teaspoons finely grated
       orange rind
    2 tablespoons strained
       orange juice
    9 egg whites
    ¼ cup sugar
    3 tablespoons orange-flavored
       liqueur
    1½ teaspoons finely grated
       orange rind

Chocolate-Dipped Candied Orange Rind

    2 oranges
    2 cups water
    2 cups sugar
       Sugar
    1 to 2 ounces semisweet
       chocolate

Chocolate Glaze

    ¼ cup unsalted butter
    6 ounces semisweet or bitter-
       sweet dark chocolate

Orange Chantilly Cream

    1 teaspoon unflavored gelatin
    2 tablespoons cold water
    1½ cups whipping cream
    ¼ cup sifted confectioners' sugar
    1 tablespoon orange-flavored
       liqueur

1. Prepare Chocolate-Dipped Candied Orange Rind. Preheat oven to 350° F. Butter and lightly flour two 10- by 2-inch cake pans or two 9½- by 3-inch springform pans. Line bottoms with circles of waxed paper.

2. Finely grind walnuts (one cup at a time with 1 tablespoon of the bread crumbs) in food processor or small jar of electric blender. Bread crumbs and ground walnuts combined should equal 4 cups. (See "How to Peel and Grind Nuts," page 67.)

3. In large bowl of electric mixer, lightly beat egg yolks. Gradually add the ¾ cup sugar and beat to the ribbon stage (see glossary, pages 122–123). Beat in orange rind and orange juice. Stir in walnut/bread crumb mixture.

4. In a large bowl, beat the egg whites until they form peaks; gradually add the ¼ cup sugar and beat until they are stiff but still glossy. Stir one fourth of the whites into the batter to lighten it. Gently fold in the remaining whites. Whites should be completely incorporated but not deflated.

5. Divide the batter equally between the two cake pans. Bake until cake is springy to the touch and begins to pull away from the sides of the cake pan (30 to 40 minutes). Cool in pan 5 minutes, then remove sides of pans and allow to finish cooling on wire racks.

6. *To assemble cake:* Make Chocolate Glaze. Split each cake layer in half horizontally with a long, serrated knife. Place one layer on cake plate; brush with 2 teaspoons orange-flavored liqueur. Spread one third of Chocolate Glaze evenly over cake and sprinkle ½ teaspoon orange rind over glaze. Repeat these steps for the next two layers. Top with fourth layer of cake; brush with remaining orange-flavored liqueur. Make Orange Chantilly Cream and use it to ice sides and top of the cake. Place remaining Orange Chantilly Cream in a pastry bag fitted with an open-star tip. Decorate border with rosettes of cream or a chain of shells. Refrigerate until ready to serve. When ready to serve, place a piece of Chocolate-Dipped Candied Orange Rind in the center of each rosette to mark each slice.

Serves 10 to 12.

Chocolate-Dipped Candied Orange Rind

1. Cut oranges in half; scoop out orange segments, leaving pith and rind intact. Cut rind into ¼-inch-wide strips. Place the strips in saucepan; cover with cold water and bring to a boil. Boil 5 minutes. Drain and repeat this process twice more to remove bitterness from rind. Combine the water with sugar in a saucepan; stir over medium heat until sugar dissolves. Add drained orange rind to sugar syrup; simmer until rind becomes translucent, about 45 minutes. Remove rind from syrup with slotted spoon. Toss in sugar and spread out on baking sheets lined with waxed paper. Allow to dry overnight. Store in airtight container when dry.

2. Cut candied rind into 1-inch pieces. Melt chocolate. Dip one end of each piece of candied rind in chocolate; place on waxed paper until chocolate hardens. May be covered and stored in a cool, dry place until ready to use.

Chocolate Glaze Clarify the butter. (To clarify butter, melt butter and use only the clear yellow oil. Discard the white milk sediment that settles to the bottom of the pan.) Melt chocolate over hot (not boiling) water. Remove from heat and stir in clarified (tepid) butter. Cool mixture to tepid (86° F).

Orange Chantilly Cream Soften gelatin in the cold water; stir over hot water (in a double boiler) until gelatin dissolves; cool until syrupy. Beat whipping cream until slightly thickened; add dissolved gelatin, confectioners' sugar, and orange-flavored liqueur. Continue beating until cream holds soft peaks that hold their form when beaters are lifted from bowl. Cream should look soft and glossy (do not overbeat).

WORKING WITH CHOCOLATE

Chocolate is an ingredient with many qualities and many uses. Here we work with melted chocolate to create a variety of decorations. The Chocolate Ruffle Torte on page 34 is an example of how the ribbon and ruffle can be used.

All chocolate work should be done at a cool time of the day, in a cool room. Handle chocolate quickly and lightly to avoid melting. These techniques are not easy for people with hot hands.

Tempering is a method of heating (melting) and cooling chocolate that ensures that the chocolate will re-harden with a shiny, unstreaked surface. Chocolate should always be tempered if it is to be used to coat the outside of a pastry or to form decorations. The best kind of chocolate to use for this purpose is a semisweet coating chocolate (also called *couverture*).

Coating chocolate melts to a better coating and spreading consistency than regular baking chocolate because it has a higher cocoa butter content. In its original, un-melted form, coating chocolate contains cocoa butter made up of stable fat crystals. If you melt and re-cool the chocolate without tempering it, some of the fat crystals may recrystallize as unstable crystals. The unstable fat crystals rise to the surface of the chocolate and form dull gray streaks (called fat bloom). The process of tempering melted choco-late promotes the formation of stable fat crystals and prevents the occur-rence of fat bloom.

If coating chocolate is unavail-able, use a good-quality semisweet or bittersweet chocolate with a high cocoa butter content. Many brands of European chocolate bars can be used in place of coating chocolate.

To make the chocolate ribbon and ruffles for the Chocolate Ruffle Torte on page 34, melt and temper 1 pound of semisweet chocolate.

To Melt Chocolate When melting chocolate by itself for any purpose, it is best to chop it into small pieces. Place the chopped chocolate in the top of a double boiler or in a stainless steel bowl over a pan of hot (not boiling) water; adjust the heat so the water remains just below a simmer. The bowl should fit snugly over the pan so no steam can escape around the bowl. If the water boils or if the bowl is too small for the pan, steam will rise and could cause the chocolate to seize and stiffen into an unmeltable mass.

Stir until the chocolate is just melted. The melting point of semi-sweet or bittersweet chocolate is 95° F to 100° F. Remove from heat when chocolate reaches this tempera-ture and is just melted.

To Temper Chocolate Finely grate a few ounces of unmelted semi-sweet or bittersweet coating choco-late. You will need 1 tablespoon grated chocolate for every 4 ounces of chocolate to be tempered. When the chopped chocolate is com-pletely melted, remove from heat and stir in the finely grated chocolate, 1 tablespoon at a time, stirring vigor-ously after each addition, until chocolate reaches 86° F (see photo above). Test with an instant-read thermometer. The chocolate can then be used to form chocolate ruffles, ribbons, leaves, and other decorations.

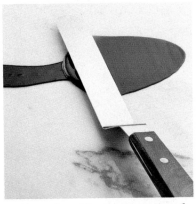

1. *To make a thin chocolate sheet for a ruffle: Refrigerate a piece of marble for several hours or place a rimmed baking sheet filled with ice on top of marble for 30 minutes to chill it. (Chocolate can be spread on the back of a baking sheet but the ruffles will not look as shiny when finished.) Dry the marble with paper towels. Pour an inch-wide strip of melted and tempered chocolate on ice cold marble. Use swift, smooth, even strokes with a flexible metal spatula to spread chocolate into a thin sheet about 3 inches wide and 10 inches long.*

2. *To form a fan-shaped ruffle: When the chocolate begins to set but is still pliable, slide a wide-bladed putty knife under right edge of chocolate. To form a fan-shaped ruffle, push chocolate toward left side of marble by moving the putty knife from right to left (flexing wrist back and forth as you push). Use index finger and thumb of left hand to gather chocolate into a ruffle as you go along. Transfer ruffle to a waxed paper–lined baking sheet and place in refrigerator immediately.*

3. *To form a ribbon to wrap a cake: Cut out a sheet of waxed paper that is slightly wider than the cake is tall and is as long as the cake's circumference. With a flexible metal spatula, spread a thin layer of melted and tempered chocolate on this waxed paper. When the chocolate begins to set but is still pliable, place one end of the strip against the cake (with the wet chocolate toward the cake). Wrap rest of chocolate strip around cake so it rests smoothly against sides of cake. Press top edge of chocolate down onto top of cake. Chill in refrigerator until chocolate is firm and waxed paper peels away easily.*

4. *For the Chocolate Ruffle Torte, make enough ruffles to cover the top of the cake in an overlapping rose-petal design. Rechill marble as necessary. Store ruffles between pieces of waxed paper in a pan in refrigerator until ready to place on cake (cover top of pan with plastic wrap).*

Chocolate Leaves *Choose thick, waxy plant leaves with visible veins. Paint melted and tempered chocolate evenly on underside of leaves. Chill in refrigerator until chocolate is firm. Slide fingernail between leaf and chocolate near stem to loosen chocolate from leaf. Pull leaf away from chocolate. Use these delicate leaves to decorate all sorts of cakes.*

Chocolate Curls *It is easiest to produce chocolate curls from a 4-ounce or larger bar of chocolate (at room temperature). Scrape the long side of the bar with a potato peeler. When chocolate is just the right temperature, this will produce nice chocolate curls. If chocolate is too cold, you will end up with short chocolate shavings or shredded chocolate.*

ALMOND MERINGUE CAKE
Dacquoise

Three layers of crisp almond meringue are filled with Chocolate and Praline Buttercream or Coffee and Chocolate Buttercream and decorated with a border of buttercream rosettes. It's best to make meringues during dry weather. Meringues are very hard to dry out in humid weather and often remain sticky after hours of baking.

> 2 cups plus 1 tablespoon sifted confectioners' sugar
> 1⅓ cups finely ground almonds (almond meal)
> 6 egg whites, at room temperature
> ⅛ teaspoon cream of tartar
> 3 cups Buttercream Icing (see page 23)

1. Preheat oven to 200° F. Line two 11- by 17-inch baking sheets with parchment paper. Draw two 8-inch circles on the back of one piece of parchment paper and one 8-inch circle on the other. If you have a large pastry bag, fit it with a ⅝-inch plain tube tip.

2. Combine half the sugar with the almond meal; set aside.

3. Beat egg whites until foamy. Add cream of tartar and continue beating until the whites begin to hold stiff peaks. Gradually add remaining sugar, 2 tablespoons at a time, and beat until whites hold stiff, glossy peaks. (Do not overbeat or whites will become dry and dull.)

4. Fold almond meal mixture into the whites. Fill pastry bag half full with meringue. Pipe out three 8-inch solid circles of meringue onto the parchment-lined baking sheets, refilling bag as necessary. If you do not have a pastry bag, spread meringue evenly on the parchment inside each of the three circles. Bake until meringue is crisp (2 to 2½ hours).

If you are using a gas oven with a pilot light, you may bake the meringues until they are set (about 1 hour) and then turn off oven and leave them to dry in the oven overnight or until crisp. Remove meringues from oven; cool briefly on wire racks. Wrap in plastic wrap and store in an airtight container until ready to use.

5. *To assemble the cake:* For an even-sided cake, carefully trim each layer of meringue to form an 8-inch circle. Use a sharp knife to avoid cracking the meringue. There are two ways to fill the layers with buttercream. You may either spread it on with a knife, or decoratively pipe it onto each layer with a pastry bag fitted with an open-star tip.

A classic *dacquoise* often has the buttercream piped onto the bottom two layers, with the sides left plain to reveal the swirls of buttercream inside. Decorate the top with stars and rosettes of contrasting buttercream. Small, whole, toasted hazelnuts or almonds could decorate the center of each rosette.

Serves 8.

Alternate Assembly Spread buttercream on the first two layers. Place third layer on top. Ice sides. Press toasted, chopped nuts or praline powder onto the sides of the cake. Dust top with confectioners' sugar or decorate with rosettes.

Mousse Meringue Cake Make Chocolate Mousse (see page 35). Ice the first two layers of meringue with mousse. Place third layer of meringue on top. Ice sides with mousse. Press chopped, toasted slivered almonds on sides of cake. Lightly dust top with confectioners' sugar. Cover and chill until ready to serve.

CHOCOLATE RUFFLE TORTE

Your efforts will be rewarded every time you make this stunning chocolate mousse torte.

> ¾ cup unsalted butter, softened
> ¾ cup sugar
> ¾ cup finely ground almonds (3 oz)
> 6 ounces bittersweet chocolate, melted and cooled
> 6 egg yolks
> 6 egg whites

Chocolate Mousse

> 1¼ cups whipping cream
> 6 ounces semisweet chocolate, melted and cooled
> ½ cup water
> 7 tablespoons sugar
> 4 egg yolks
> Chocolate Ribbon and Ruffles or Chocolate Curls (see page 33)

1. Preheat oven to 350° F. Butter and lightly flour two 8- by 2-inch round cake pans (see the Pan Substitution chart, page 10, if you don't have pans this size). Line bottom of each with a circle of waxed paper.

2. In large electric mixer bowl, cream butter with half of the sugar until light. Add almonds and beat until light. Beat in melted chocolate.

3. Add egg yolks, one at a time, beating well after each addition; beat until light and fluffy.

4. Beat egg whites in a separate bowl until they begin to hold peaks. Gradually add remaining sugar and beat until stiff but still glossy.

5. Stir one fourth of the egg whites into the chocolate mixture to lighten batter. Then gently fold in remaining whites. Whites should be completely incorporated but not deflated.

6. Divide the batter equally between the two pans and gently smooth top of batter. Bake for 30 to 40 minutes or until done. Cool in pans 10 minutes, then turn out onto wire racks to finish cooling. This cake tends to sink in the middle as it cools. Trim top with serrated knife to create even layers.

7. Prepare Chocolate Mousse.

8. Place one layer on a cardboard cake circle that is ⅛ inch smaller than the cake. Spread half of Chocolate Mousse over this layer. Set next layer on top of mousse. Spread remaining Chocolate Mousse on sides and top of cake. Refrigerate until mousse is firm (about 45 minutes).

9. Decorate cake with Chocolate Ribbon and Ruffles (see page 33), or sprinkle top of cake with Chocolate Curls (see page 33).

Serves 8.

Chocolate Mousse Whip the cream until it holds soft peaks. Refrigerate.

Melt chocolate; cool to tepid. Combine water and sugar in saucepan. Bring to a boil to dissolve sugar. Boil 1 minute. Measure out ½ cup hot syrup. Place egg yolks in a deep, 4- to 5-quart stainless steel bowl. Whisk in hot syrup. Continue whisking in one direction (either clockwise or counterclockwise) over a double boiler until the mixture holds soft peaks (5 to 7 minutes). Beat yolks off heat with electric mixer or by hand until they are cool. Stir in melted, tepid chocolate. Fold in one eighth of the whipped cream. Gradually fold in remaining whipped cream. If you fold the cream in too quickly, it will cause the chocolate to harden and form chocolate chips.

Chocolate Ruffle Torte, adorned with pleats of rich chocolate, is a cake that borders on being a work of art. Best of all, it tastes more wonderful than it looks.

BUNDT CAKES

Bundt cakes take their name from the decorative ring-shaped pans in which they are baked. These pans are deep and round and have a hole in the center. Their curves and indentations mold the cake batter to produce a cake with an attractive sculpted exterior.

CHOCOLATE-ALMOND BUNDT CAKE

There are occasions when cakes should be slightly dry, and not too sweet. Through their simplicity they achieve an elegance. This cake is a fine example. The ground almonds and delicious morsels of semisweet chocolate hiding inside this bundt cake make it scrumptious.

      3⅓ cups sifted cake flour
      1½ tablespoons baking powder
      1½ cups finely ground blanched
           almonds
      27 tablespoons (1½ cups plus 3
           tablespoons) unsalted butter,
           softened
      1½ cups granulated sugar
       6 egg yolks
       6 egg whites
       8 ounces semisweet chocolate,
           coarsely chopped
       ⅓ cup confectioners' sugar

1. Preheat oven to 375° F. Generously butter a 12-cup bundt pan; dust with flour.

2. Sift flour and baking powder together. Stir in ground almonds; set aside.

3. In large bowl of electric mixer, cream the butter and 1 cup of the granulated sugar together; beat until light. Add the egg yolks, one at a time, beating well after each addition. Stir in flour mixture.

4. Beat egg whites in a medium bowl until they hold soft peaks. Add the remaining ½ cup granulated sugar, 1 tablespoon at a time, and beat until whites are stiff but still glossy (do not overbeat). Lighten the batter with one fourth of the whites. Then gently fold in the remaining whites.

5. Place about one fourth of the batter in the pan. Then sprinkle one third of the chocolate on the batter. Continue to fill the pan with alternating layers of batter and chocolate, ending with a layer of batter.

6. Bake 20 minutes. Reduce oven to 325° F and bake 30 minutes longer or until done. Unmold cake and cool on wire rack (decorative side up). When cake is cool, dust with confectioners' sugar.

Serves 8 to 10.

BLACKBERRY JAM CAKE

Old-fashioned jam cake is a beautiful sight, with its golden brown surface studded with shiny blackberries. Unlike most bundt cakes, this one is as light as a feather. For special occasions, fill the center with fresh blackberries and pipe whipped cream rosettes around the base of the cake.

       1 cup unsalted butter, softened
      1¾ cups sugar
       4 eggs
       1 teaspoon vanilla extract
       3 cups sifted cake flour
       1 teaspoon baking soda
      1½ teaspoons ground cinnamon
       ½ teaspoon ground nutmeg
       ½ teaspoon ground ginger
       1 cup buttermilk
       1 cup (12 oz) blackberry
           preserves
           Fresh blackberries, for
           decoration
           Whipped cream, for decoration

1. Preheat oven to 300° F. Butter and lightly flour a 10-inch tube pan or bundt pan.

2. In large bowl of electric mixer, cream butter and gradually add sugar, beating until light and fluffy. Beat in eggs one at a time. Beat in vanilla.

3. Sift together flour, soda, cinnamon, nutmeg, and ginger. Add to butter mixture alternately with buttermilk, beating after each addition. Fold in blackberry preserves.

4. Pour into pan and bake 15 minutes. Increase oven to 350° F and bake until done (40 to 50 minutes longer). Cool in pan 10 minutes. Turn out onto wire rack to finish cooling. To serve, fill center with fresh berries and pipe whipped cream around base of cake.

Serves 10.

Variations This cake is also delicious when made with other flavors of jams and preserves. Simply replace 1 cup of blackberry preserves with 1 cup of another berry preserve or jam. Strawberry, raspberry, olallieberry, loganberry, or blueberry preserves are excellent substitutes. Decorate the cake with fresh berries to match the preserves you choose.

   This cake may also be baked in three 8-inch layer-cake pans. Ice with Whipped Cream Icing (see Pecan-Applesauce Cake, page 44).

Old-fashioned Blackberry Jam Cake is perfect for breakfast, lunch, or dinner. Decorate with rosettes of whipped cream and fresh berries.

WHIPPING CREAM

Whip cream just before using because whipped cream tends to deflate when held in refrigerator for several hours. Whip cold whipping cream in a well-chilled bowl with chilled beaters or whisk. Beat cream to desired consistency. (If cream is beaten beyond soft peak stage, it will become lumpy and eventually turn into butter.) Slightly over-beaten cream can be revived by adding some unwhipped cream and stirring until smooth. To sweeten or flavor whipped cream, see Chantilly Cream, page 59.

CRÈME FRAÎCHE

Crème Fraîche can be used in place of whipped cream in Chantilly Cream, chocolate mousse, Bavarian creams, and others. Crème Fraîche is a little more tart than whipped cream, giving things it is used in a less sweet taste. Raw cream and raw buttermilk thicken more quickly than ultrapasteurized dairy products.

Heat 2 cups whipping cream to 100° F. (Use an instant-read thermometer to test.) Remove from heat and place in a glass jar with loose-fitting lid. Stir in ¼ cup buttermilk. Allow to stand at warm room temperature (70° F to 75° F) until cream has thickened (24 to 36 hours). Refrigerate after cream has thickened.

Makes 2 cups.

AMOR POLENTA
Cornmeal pound cake

Cornmeal and ground almonds give this Italian pound cake its distinctive taste and texture—very crisp on the outside, and moist yet crumbly on the inside. It is delicious plain or can be served with Chantilly Cream and fresh berries.

    9   *tablespoons unsalted butter*
    ¾   *cup granulated sugar*
    3   *egg yolks*
    1   *teaspoon vanilla extract*
    1   *cup plus 2 tablespoons sifted
        cake flour*
    1   *teaspoon baking powder*
    ⅔   *cup yellow cornmeal*
    1   *cup finely ground blanched
        almonds (4 oz)*
    3   *egg whites*
    2   *tablespoons granuated sugar
        Confectioners' sugar, for
        decoration*

1. Preheat oven to 325° F. Butter a 12- by 4-inch ribbed deerback pan (see page 10) or any 4- to 5-cup baking pan. Dust with cornmeal.

2. In medium bowl of electric mixer, cream butter; gradually add the ¾ cup granulated sugar and beat until light. Add egg yolks, one at a time, beating after each addition. Add vanilla.

3. Sift flour and baking powder together. Combine with cornmeal and almonds. Add dry ingredients to butter mixture and beat until well blended.

4. Beat egg whites until they form soft peaks. Add the 2 tablespoons granulated sugar and beat until stiff but still glossy. Stir half of the whites into the yolk mixture to lighten the batter. Gently fold in the remaining whites.

5. Spread batter evenly in pan and bake until cake tester comes out clean (about 1 hour). Cool in pan 5 minutes. Invert cake on wire rack, remove cake pan. Dust immediately with confectioners' sugar.

Serves 8.

CHOCOLATE CREAM CAKE

Here is a chocolate marble cake designed to be eaten with your fingers. You'll love taking it on picnics or in box lunches.

    4   *ounces semisweet chocolate,
        coarsely chopped*
    2¼ *cups sifted cake flour*
    1½ *teaspoons baking powder*
    ¾   *cup granulated sugar*
    1   *cup whipping cream*
    2   *tablespoons lemon juice*
    2   *extra-large eggs
        Confectioners' sugar, for
        decoration*

1. Preheat oven to 375° F. Butter and flour a 4½-inch by 9½-inch by 3-inch (deep) loaf pan. Line bottom of pan with parchment paper.

2. Melt chocolate in a bowl over hot (not boiling) water. When chocolate is just melted, remove from heat; cool 10 minutes.

3. Sift flour with baking powder twice.

4. Combine granulated sugar, cream, and lemon juice in a medium bowl. Add eggs, one at a time, beating well after each addition.

5. Divide the batter into 2 medium bowls. Stir the melted chocolate into half of the batter. Stir half of the flour into each half of the batter. Fill the loaf pan, alternating layers of chocolate and vanilla batter. To create a marbled effect, run a knife through the batter in a figure eight pattern.

6. Bake 20 minutes. Reduce oven to 350° F and bake 20 to 30 minutes longer or until done. Turn out onto wire rack to finish cooling. When cool, sift a light layer of confectioners' sugar on top.

Serves 8.

PEAR-WALNUT CROSTADA

Memories of Italian pastry are dominated by these wonderful cakelike crostadas. Fresh, ripe pears and crunchy walnuts are dusted with cocoa and baked in a light pound cake batter with a crisp crostada crust.

 4 *ripe pears (Anjou or Bartlett)*
 2 *teaspoons lemon juice*
 2 *tablespoons flour*
 4 *egg yolks*
 1 *cup granulated sugar*
 18 *tablespoons unsalted butter, softened*
 2¼ *cups cake flour*
 1 *tablespoon baking powder*
 1 *teaspoon finely grated orange rind*
 1 *tablespoon dark rum*
 4 *egg whites*
 ¼ *cup granulated sugar*
 1 *egg white, lightly beaten*
 ⅔ *cup coarsely chopped walnuts*
 1 *heaping tablespoon unsweetened cocoa powder*
  Confectioners' sugar, for decoration

Crostada Pastry

 1¾ *cups flour*
 1 *teaspoon baking powder*
 ¼ *teaspoon salt*
 ½ *cup sugar*
 ½ *teaspoon finely grated lemon rind*
 ½ *teaspoon finely grated orange rind*
 1 *egg*
 ⅔ *cup cold butter*

1. Line a 9-inch springform pan (or a 9- by 3-inch cake circle positioned on a baking sheet) with Crostada Pastry. Pastry should be rolled out to a 12 inch diameter in order to accommodate the 3-inch depth. Blind-bake crust until partially baked (see page 60 for technique).

2. Peel, core, and quarter pears; toss them in lemon juice, then toss pears in the 2 tablespoons flour; set aside.

3. Beat egg yolks and the 1 cup granulated sugar in a large bowl until light; beat in butter.

4. Sift the 2¼ cups flour and baking powder together; stir into yolk mixture. Stir in orange rind and rum.

5. Beat the 4 egg whites until they hold soft peaks; beat in the ¼ cup granulated sugar, one tablespoon at a time, and continue beating until stiff but still glossy (do not overbeat). Stir one fourth of the whites into the yolk mixture to lighten batter. Gently fold in the remaining whites.

6. Preheat oven to 350° F. Brush inside of partially baked crostada shell with the lightly beaten egg white to moisture-proof shell. Spread half of the batter in the bottom of the crostada shell. Arrange quartered pears in a single layer on the batter. Sprinkle the walnuts over the pears. Then sift the cocoa powder evenly over the nuts. Spread the remaining batter on top. Cover the edges of the crostada shell with strips of foil to prevent overbrowning. Bake until done (45 to 60 minutes). Cool on a wire rack. Dust with confectioners' sugar. Unmold and serve at room temperature.

Serves 12.

Variation For a quicker version that is nearly as delicious, this cake can be made without the pastry crust. Bake in a 9-inch springform pan and reduce the number of pears used from 4 to 3.

Crostada Pastry

To Make by Hand

1. Sift flour and baking powder onto work surface; form a well in the center. Combine salt, sugar, lemon rind, orange rind, and egg in the well; stir to mix.

2. Pound butter with a rolling pin to soften; work butter into egg mixture (with fingertips or fork) until partially mixed. Then cut the wet ingredients into the flour with a pastry scraper or cutter.

3. Gather the dough into a rough ball. The dough will not really stick together at this point and it will look dry. To create a smooth dough, quickly push pieces of the dough against the work surface with the heel of your hand. When the dough is smooth and pliable, press into a ball, wrap well, and refrigerate 1 hour or until firm.

4. Roll out the dough on a lightly floured surface to form a circle that is ⅛ inch thick and 1½ inches larger in diameter than your pan (see page 72). Wrap well and refrigerate 1 hour. Tart shell may be frozen at this point.

Food Processor Method

Combine salt, sugar, lemon rind, orange rind, egg, and softened butter in bowl of food processor fitted with metal blade; process with 4 one-second pulses. Sift flour and baking powder together and add all at once; process with 8 to 10 one-second pulses. Remove dough from processor, gather into a rough ball, and continue with step 3 above.

LE WEEKEND
Lemon-orange pound cake

Make this cake on the weekend and it will keep all week long. Serve it plain any time of day or serve it for dessert with fresh fruit and Chantilly Cream. Prepare the Crème Fraîche at least one day before you make the cake.

    4 eggs
 1¼ cups sugar
    ½ teaspoon salt
    ⅔ cup Crème Fraîche (see page 38) or whipping cream
    2 teaspoons finely grated lemon rind
    2 cups sifted flour (scant)
 1¼ teaspoons baking powder
    ½ cup unsalted butter, melted and cooled
    2 tablespoons rum
    ¼ cup orange-flavored liqueur

Lemon-Orange Glaze

    ¼ cup strained orange juice
    ¼ cup strained lemon juice
    1 teaspoon finely grated lemon rind
 2½ cups sifted confectioners' sugar

1. Preheat oven to 325° F. Butter and lightly flour a 9- by 4-inch loaf pan. Line bottom of pan with parchment paper.

2. In medium bowl of electric mixer, lightly beat eggs. Gradually add sugar and salt to eggs and beat until light and fluffy. Beat in Crème Fraîche and lemon rind.

3. Sift flour and baking powder together. Add to egg mixture and beat until smooth. Fold in butter and rum. Pour batter into pan and bake until done (1 to 1½ hours). Prepare Lemon-Orange Glaze.

4. Remove cake from pan while hot and place right side up on a wire rack positioned over a rimmed baking sheet. Pierce top of cake in several places with a thin wooden skewer. Brush surface of cake with orange-flavored liqueur. Brush some of the glaze on sides and top of cake. Spoon glaze over cake until all glaze is used up. Cover cake with a dome or a bowl until cool. Wrap and store at room temperature.

Serves 8 to 10.

Lemon-Orange Glaze In a saucepan combine orange juice, lemon juice, lemon rind, and sugar. Stir over medium heat until sugar is dissolved. Set aside.

CARROT SPICE CAKE

Recipes like this one will certainly revive the carrot cake craze.

 1⅓ cups unsalted butter
 1¾ cups sugar
    4 eggs
    2 cups flour
    2 teaspoons baking soda
    1 teaspoon ground cinnamon
    ½ teaspoon ground allspice
    ¼ teaspoon ground nutmeg
    ¼ teaspoon ground cloves
    3 cups grated carrots (approximately 1 lb)
 1¼ cups chopped walnuts
    ¼ cup golden raisins
    ¼ cup coarsely chopped walnuts, for decoration

Cream Cheese Icing

6 ounces cream cheese, softened
¼ cup unsalted butter, softened
2 cups sifted confectioners' sugar
2 teaspoons lemon juice

1. Preheat oven to 325° F. Butter and lightly flour a 9- by 13-inch baking pan.

2. In large bowl, cream butter; gradually add sugar and beat until light. Add eggs one at a time, beating after each addition.

3. Sift flour, baking soda, cinnamon, allspice, nutmeg, and cloves together. Add to butter mixture and stir until well blended. Stir in carrots, the 1¼ cups walnuts, and raisins.

4. Spread batter evenly in pan. Bake until done (45 to 55 minutes). Cool in pan on wire rack. Spread Cream Cheese Icing on cool cake. Sprinkle the ¼ cup walnuts on top. Serve at room temperature.

Serves 12.

Cream Cheese Icing Cream cream cheese with butter. Add confectioners' sugar and lemon juice; beat until smooth.

These five pound and bundt cakes are moist and delectable. Clockwise from left to right: Chocolate Cream Cake (page 38), Chocolate-Almond Bundt Cake (page 36), Amor Polenta (page 38), Le Weekend, and Pear-Walnut Crostada (page 39).

41

DARK FRUITCAKE IN CANDIED GRAPEFRUIT HALVES

This fruitcake, made of dried fruits rather than candied fruits, has a delightful flavor. The fruitcake recipe yields approximately 8 cups of batter and may be baked in any size tins. If you don't have time to make the candied grapefruit halves, bake little cakes in small, fluted brioche pans, 1½- to 2-cup charlotte tins, or small loaf pans.

- ¾ cup dried currants
- ½ cup chopped dried apples
- ¾ cup chopped dried apricots
- ¾ cup chopped pitted dates
- ¾ cup seedless raisins
- ½ cup chopped dried figs
- 1 cup mincemeat
- 2 cups chopped nuts (pecans, hazelnuts, or walnuts)
- ¼ cup dark rum
- ¼ cup good-quality bourbon
- 2 teaspoons instant espresso or 4 teaspoons instant coffee
- ¼ cup dark molasses (preferably Brer Rabbit)
- ½ teaspoon finely ground cardamom seed
- ¼ teaspoon each ground cloves, allspice, cinnamon, and mace
- ¾ teaspoon salt
- 1¾ cup flour
- 2 teaspoons baking powder
- ½ cup unsalted butter
- 1¼ cups light brown sugar
- 1 tablespoon vanilla extract
- 3 extra-large eggs
  Nut halves, candied orange or grapefruit rind, cedro, dried fruits, glacé fruit, for decoration
  Rum or brandy, for soaking cakes

Candied Grapefruit Halves (optional)

- 4 large ruby-red grapefruits with firm, unblemished skins
- 8 cups sugar
- 4 cups water
- ⅔ cup light corn syrup
  Extra sugar to roll grapefruit halves in

1. Prepare Candied Grapefruit Halves (if used) 1 day before cakes are to be baked. Also macerate (soak) dried fruits and nuts the day before.

2. *To macerate fruit and nuts:* Place the currants, apples, apricots, dates, raisins, and figs (chopped into fairly small pieces) in a large bowl. Pour about 6 cups boiling water over fruits, stir, and allow to stand 2 minutes; drain off water. Return softened fruit to bowl and add mincemeat, nuts, rum, bourbon, espresso, molasses, cardamom, cloves, allspice, cinnamon, mace, and salt. Stir well, cover, and allow to stand at least 12 hours at room temperature.

3. Preheat oven to 275° F. Butter and flour baking pans (two 8-inch round pans) or place drained Candied Grapefruit Halves on buttered baking sheets.

4. Sift flour with baking powder; stir into the fruit mixture. In large bowl of electric mixer, cream the butter and sugar together until light; add the vanilla. Beat in eggs, one at a time. Add the fruit mixture a little at a time, stirring after each addition until the batter is smooth.

5. Fill grapefruit halves or cake pans almost to the top with batter. Decorate the top of each cake with a design made with nut halves, candied orange or grapefruit rind, sliced cedro, sliced dried fruits, or glacé fruits. Bake until a skewer inserted in center comes out clean (1 hour). The cake(s) will rise only slightly and will crack.

6. Remove cake(s) from oven and roll Candied Grapefruit Halves (if used) in sugar. Otherwise, turn cakes out of pans and cool on wire racks. Pour a little rum or brandy on each cake. Cool to room temperature. Wrap each cake in rum-soaked cheesecloth and place in a covered cake tin. Pour a little rum on each cake once a week until ready to give as gifts or serve to guests. Fruitcake will keep for about a year.

7. Serve at room temperature in small slices with port and either Stilton or Roquefort cheese. The candied grapefruit containers are also delicious.

Makes 8 small fruitcakes or two 8-inch cakes.

Candied Grapefruit Halves

1. Cut each grapefruit in half and squeeze juice or remove fruit for another use. Carefully scrape out as much of the white pith as possible without piercing the skin. Place the grapefruit halves in a pot, cover with cold water, and bring to a boil. Reduce heat and simmer 10 minutes; drain. Repeat this process 2 more times to soften the pith and remove bitterness from rind and pith.

2. After simmering the rinds three times, scrape out more of the pith with a spoon. Drain grapefruits upside down on a rack. Meanwhile dissolve sugar in water in a very large, heavy pot; stir corn syrup into sugar syrup. Bring this mixture to a boil over medium-high heat, washing down any sugar crystals that cling to the sides of the pan with a pastry brush dipped in cold water. Boil for 30 minutes or until candy thermometer reaches 226° F. Place drained halves in syrup and cook until syrup reaches 228° F. Remove from heat and allow grapefruits to sit overnight in syrup. The next day, remove from syrup and drain. (If the sugar has crystallized, you can warm the syrup to reliquefy the sugar before removing the rinds.) Fill the rinds with batter and bake.

CHOCOLATE WALNUT-CARAMEL CAKE

Here's a cake that is a tart, a cake, and a candy bar all in one. A thick caramel-walnut center is wrapped in buttery Sweet Tart Pastry and covered with a thin layer of chocolate.

    1½ cups sugar
    1   cup water
    1   cup whipping cream (scant)
    2½ cups walnut halves
    7   tablespoons unsalted butter, softened
    1   egg white, lightly beaten
    ½   cup apricot preserves
    6   ounces semisweet chocolate
    4   tablespoons unsalted butter
        Walnut halves, for decoration (optional)

Sweet Tart Pastry

    10 tablespoons cold butter
    4   egg yolks
    ¼   teaspoon salt
    ½   cup sugar
    1   teaspoon vanilla extract
    1¾ cups flour

1. Prepare Sweet Tart Pastry. Line bottom of an 8-inch-diameter, 1½-inch-deep, round cake pan with a circle of parchment paper. Brush sides of pan with melted butter. Roll out the larger piece of dough (10 oz) into a circle ⅛ inch thick and 10 inches in diameter (see "Rolling Out Tart Pastry," page 72). Mold dough to bottom and sides of pan with gentle finger pressure or a small ball of dough. If the dough breaks as you are trying to fit it into the pan, just press it into the pan all around in an even layer. Patch holes with small pieces of dough. The bottom and sides of the pan must be covered with an even layer of pastry; none of the pan should show through (or the filling will leak out later). Wrap pastry shell and refrigerate while you make the filling. Roll out the smaller

piece of dough into a circle ⅛ inch thick and 8 inches in diameter. Prick all over with a fork. Place on waxed paper-lined baking sheet; cover and refrigerate.

2. Place sugar and water in a 2½-quart saucepan; stir until sugar dissolves and syrup comes to a boil. Boil, without stirring, until sugar is a light caramel color (320° F on a candy thermometer). Remove from heat.

3. Add cream and stir to blend. Then stir in walnuts and the 7 tablespoons soft butter. Return to heat and bring to a boil, stirring constantly. Boil gently until the syrup reaches 225° F on candy thermometer (see page 24). Remove from heat. Cool for 40 minutes, stirring occasionally. Preheat oven to 375° F.

4. Brush inside of pastry-lined cake pan with a thin layer of egg white to moisture-proof shell. Spread cooled caramel filling in bottom of shell. Trim sides of pastry shell to ⅛ inch above filling. Moisten top edge of pastry shell. Place pastry lid on top; press to seal at edges.

5. Bake until pastry is golden brown (40 to 50 minutes). Remove from oven; cool in pan 30 minutes. Turn out onto wire rack to cool. (Be careful when turning cake out of pan. The caramel is still very hot.) Cool completely before covering with chocolate glaze.

6. Heat apricot preserves until melted and bubbly. Strain to remove pieces of fruit. Brush entire surface of cooled pastry with warm preserves.

7. *To make chocolate glaze:* Break chocolate into small pieces and place in a small stainless steel bowl over a pot of hot (not boiling) water. Melt the 4 tablespoons butter in small saucepan, and skim off the white foam that rises to the top. When chocolate is just melted, stir in clarified butter (discard any white solids left in bottom of butter pan). Set aside until chocolate is 86° F (use instant-read thermometer to test).

8. Slide cake onto a cardboard cake circle (a cardboard circle covered with foil) that is slightly smaller in diameter than the cake. Place cake on a wire rack over a rimmed baking sheet (to catch excess chocolate glaze). Pour chocolate glaze (at 86° F; if glaze cools too much, warm it briefly over a pot of hot water) over cake and, using a narrow metal spatula, quickly spread it evenly over the top and sides of the cake. To decorate, place walnut halves (if used) on top (evenly spaced) at edge of cake. Allow chocolate to set to firm consistency before serving.

9. Store cake at cool room temperature. If refrigerated, allow to warm to room temperature before serving. Serve in 1-inch wedges. Cake is very rich.

Serves 12.

Sweet Tart Pastry Pound cold butter with rolling pin to soften slightly. Place egg yolks, salt, sugar, vanilla, and butter in bowl of food processor fitted with a metal blade; process using 4 one-second pulses until partially mixed. Add flour all at once and process with 6 to 8 one-second pulses until dough begins to clump (but does not form a ball). Gather dough into a rough mound on work surface. Work small portions of the dough against the work surface with the heel of your hand (pushing dough away from you). Press pieces of dough into a ball. Divide ball into two pieces: one piece that is less than two thirds of the dough (10 oz) for the bottom crust, and one piece that is just over one third of the dough (8 oz) for the top. Refrigerate 2 hours or until firm. To make tart pastry by hand, see page 72.

CHOCOLATE MOUSSE CAKE

For the lightest confection imaginable, try this flourless chocolate mousse cake. Half of the batter is baked to form the cake base and the other half is chilled to form the mousse topping.

    8   egg yolks
    ⅔   cup sugar
    9   ounces semisweet chocolate,
        melted and cooled
    8   egg whites
    2   tablespoons sugar
    2   cups Chantilly Cream
        (see page 59)
        Fresh raspberries and blue-
        berries or Chocolate
        Curls, for decoration

1. Preheat oven to 350° F. Lightly butter and flour the sides of a 10-inch-diameter, 3-inch-deep, round springform pan; line bottom with a circle of waxed paper.

2. Place egg yolks in a large bowl; gradually add the ⅔ cup sugar; beat until light and fluffy. Beat in melted chocolate.

3. Beat egg whites in a large bowl until they hold soft peaks. Add the 2 tablespoons sugar and beat until whites hold stiff peaks but are still glossy. Fold whites into chocolate mixture.

4. Divide batter in half. Cover and refrigerate half of the batter. Pour the remaining batter into springform pan; bake 20 to 25 minutes. Cool in pan on wire rack.

5. When cake is completely cool, spread cold mousse batter on it. Refrigerate 1 hour.

6. To serve, remove sides of pan and spread or pipe a layer of Chantilly Cream on top and sides of cake. Decorate with fresh berries or Chocolate Curls (see page 33).

Serves 8 to 10.

WHITE AND DARK CHOCOLATE HAZELNUT CAKE

Everyone loves cakes with lots of thin layers stacked one upon the other. This striking ribbon effect is created simply and easily here with a delicious hazelnut cake and buttercream split into two batches, one flavored with white chocolate and one with dark. This elegant cake is a lot easier to make than it looks.

    1¼ cups skinned, finely ground
        hazelnuts (see page 67)
    ⅓   cup sugar
    3   extra-large eggs
    1   teaspoon vanilla extract
    3   extra-large egg whites
    ⅛   teaspoon cream of tartar
    ¼   cup sugar
    ⅓   cup sifted cake flour
    ½   cup water
    ⅓   cup sugar
    1   to 2 tablespoons dark rum
    3   cups Buttercream Icing
        (see page 23)
    ½   cup whipping cream
    3   ounces semisweet dark
        chocolate, melted and
        cooled to tepid
    5   ounces white chocolate, melted
        and cooled to tepid
    ½   cup powdered Praline (see
        page 24) or finely chopped
        toasted nuts
    10 whole toasted and skinned
        hazelnuts, for decoration
        Chocolate Leaves made with
        2 ounces semisweet dipping
        chocolate (see page 33),
        for decoration

1. Preheat oven to 450° F. Butter and flour the sides of an 11- by 17-inch jellyroll pan (rimmed baking sheet). Line bottom of pan with a sheet of parchment paper cut to fit bottom of pan exactly.

2. Combine ground hazelnuts and the ⅓ cup sugar in a medium bowl. Add eggs, one at a time, beating well after each addition. Continue beating until light and thick (about 5 minutes). Beat in vanilla.

3. In a separate bowl, beat egg whites until foamy; add cream of tartar and beat until whites begin to form peaks. Add the ¼ cup sugar gradually and beat until whites hold stiff, glossy peaks (do not overbeat). Fold one fourth of the whites into the hazelnut mixture. Then fold in the flour. When flour is well incorporated, carefully fold in the remaining whites. Spread the batter evenly in pan. Bake until light brown and springy to the touch (10 minutes).

4. Cool cake in pan 5 minutes. Run a knife along edge to loosen. Remove cake from pan; slide onto wire rack, paper-side down, and cool. Cover with a clean towel while cooling. Carefully peel paper off cake. Cut the cake into four equal pieces (4 by 11 inches each). Wrap layers (separated with waxed paper) until ready to assemble cake. Cake may be frozen at this point.

5. Combine water and the ⅓ cup sugar in saucepan; bring to a boil to dissolve sugar. Cool to room temperature; flavor with rum to taste. Set aside this soaking syrup or refrigerate until ready to assemble cake.

6. Prepare Buttercream Icing. Beat the whipping cream until it holds stiff peaks. Fold into buttercream. Place just less than half of the buttercream in another bowl. Beat the semisweet dark chocolate into the smaller amount of buttercream. Beat the white chocolate into the remaining buttercream. You may also add powdered Praline to either or both of the buttercreams at this point. Refrigerate until ready to assemble cake. If buttercream hardens in refrigerator, allow to warm up to room temperature and beat until smooth. Keeps 2 to 3 days in refrigerator.

7. *To assemble cake:* Place first layer of cake on a foil-covered cardboard rectangle (just slightly smaller than 4 by 11 inches). Brush one fourth of the soaking syrup over cake to moisten it. Spread half of the dark chocolate buttercream evenly over cake.

Place second cake layer on top; brush with syrup; spread about one third of the white chocolate buttercream over this layer. Place the third layer of cake on top; brush it with syrup and spread with all but ¼ cup of the remaining dark chocolate buttercream. Place fourth layer of cake on top; brush with syrup and spread a layer of white chocolate buttercream on top and on long sides. Cover long sides of cake with powdered Praline or finely chopped toasted nuts. Refrigerate until buttercream is firm.

8. *To finish cake:* Trim a thin slice off each end to reveal layers. Pipe a decorative border on top of cake with either white or dark chocolate buttercream, using a small open-star tip. Pipe rosettes of buttercream down center of cake to mark each slice. Place a whole hazelnut in the center of each rosette. Place Chocolate Leaves decoratively on cake. Refrigerate cake. To serve, allow cake to stand at room temperature until buttercream softens slightly (1 hour).

Serves 8 to 10.

This striking dessert features thin layers of hazelnut cake with alternating layers of white and dark chocolate buttercream. Rosettes of buttercream, chocolate-dipped hazelnuts, and Chocolate Leaves decorate the top.

STRAWBERRY MIRROR CAKE

This is the perfect do-ahead dessert; it can be broken down into four simple recipes and prepared in four separate steps. The cake layers can be baked and frozen. The soaking syrup can be kept for weeks. The strawberry purée and Strawberry Juice can be prepared and either refrigerated or frozen until ready to use. Even if you do want to make this in one day, each step is quick and easy. However, it does take several hours to set after assembly.

    3   eggs
    3   egg yolks
    ¾   cup sugar
    1   teaspoon vanilla extract
    3   egg whites
    ⅛   teaspoon cream of tartar
    2   tablespoons sugar
    ⅔   cup sifted cake flour
    ½   cup water
    ⅓   cup sugar
    2   tablespoons kirsch or
        strawberry liqueur

Strawberry Bavarian Cream

    2½ tablespoons unflavored
        gelatin (2½ envelopes)
    1½ cups strained strawberry
        purée (1½ baskets)
    5   egg yolks
    ⅔   cup sugar
    1½ cups milk
    1   tablespoon lemon juice
        Several drops red food
        coloring
    1¾ cups whipping cream

Strawberry Mirror

    1   teaspoon lemon juice
    1   tablespoon kirsch
    1   tablespoon water
    1   tablespoon unflavored gelatin
        (1 envelope)
        Few drops red food coloring
        (if necessary)
        Fresh strawberries, for
        decoration (about 12 oz)

Strawberry Juice

    1½ pints ripe strawberries (18 oz)
    ¾   cup sugar
    ¾   cup water

1. Preheat oven to 450° F. Butter and flour the sides of an 11- by 17-inch jellyroll pan (rimmed baking sheet). Line bottom of pan with a sheet of parchment paper cut to fit bottom of pan exactly.

2. Beat eggs, egg yolks, and the ¾ cup sugar together in a medium bowl until thick and light (to the ribbon stage; see glossary, pages 122–123). Beat in vanilla.

3. In a separate bowl, beat the egg whites until foamy; add cream of tartar and beat until whites begin to form peaks. Add the 2 tablespoons sugar and beat until whites hold stiff, glossy peaks (do not overbeat).

4. Sift the flour over the egg yolk mixture and fold in. Stir in one fourth of the whites. Then carefully fold in the remaining whites.

5. Spread batter evenly in pan. Bake until light brown and springy to the touch (7 to 10 minutes). Cool in pan 5 minutes. Run a knife along edge to loosen. Invert cake onto a wire rack and cover with a clean dish towel while cooling. Carefully peel paper off cake. Using an inverted cake tin as a guide, cut out two 8¼-inch circles of cake. Wrap cake layers, separated with waxed paper, and set aside. Cake may be frozen at this point.

6. *To make soaking syrup:* Combine water and the ⅓ cup sugar in saucepan; bring to a boil to dissolve sugar. Cool to room temperature; flavor with liqueur. Set aside or refrigerate in glass jar until ready to use.

7. *To assemble cake:* Brush sides of 10-inch springform pan lightly with flavorless salad oil or almond oil. Cut out a cardboard circle that is exactly the same size as the bottom inside of the pan; cover cardboard circle with aluminum foil and fit into bottom of pan. Center one layer of the cake in bottom of pan. Brush the cake with some of the soaking syrup to just moisten (not drench) the cake; set aside.

8. Prepare Strawberry Bavarian Cream. Immediately pour about half of the Bavarian cream over the first layer of cake in the pan. Set the next layer of cake on top of the cream. Brush cake with soaking syrup. Pour remaining Bavarian cream over cake and smooth top of cream with spatula. Refrigerate until the cream sets (1 to 2 hours).

9. Prepare the Strawberry Mirror topping.

10. *To serve:* Wrap a hot towel around the outside of springform pan for a few minutes. Run a small sharp knife tip around the edge of the Strawberry Mirror to separate it from the sides of pan. Mirror will tear when sides are unlatched if it is stuck at any point. Slowly unlatch the pan and slide it off the cake. Slice cake in wedges and serve in upright slices.

Serves 10 to 12.

Strawberry Bavarian Cream

1. Sprinkle the gelatin over the strawberry purée in a small bowl and set aside until spongy.

2. Combine egg yolks and sugar in a bowl; beat until light. Bring milk to a boil in saucepan. Pour hot milk into yolk mixture and stir with a wooden spoon. Return this mixture to the saucepan and cook over medium heat, stirring constantly, until your finger leaves a clear trail in sauce when drawn across the back of the spoon. (Do not boil or mixture will curdle.) Immediately remove from heat and stir in softened gelatin mixture. Pour into a stainless steel bowl placed over a bowl of ice water. Stir in lemon juice and a few drops of red food coloring. Cool over ice water, stirring occasionally, until mixture thickens to the consistency of softly whipped cream.

3. While gelatin mixture is cooling, whip the whipping cream until it holds soft peaks. When the gelatin mixture resembles softly whipped cream, fold the whipped cream into the gelatin mixture.

Strawberry Mirror

For a spectacular finish for the cake, make a clear Strawberry Mirror top or one with fresh sliced strawberries set into it. If you want to use fresh strawberries, complete this last step on the same day that the cake will be served. Crowd strawberry slices together so they overlap because they tend to shrink slightly as they stand in the Strawberry Mirror. Allow mirror to chill 1 to 2 hours or until set before serving cake.

1. Prepare Strawberry Juice.

2. Place lemon juice, kirsch, and water in a small bowl. Sprinkle gelatin over this mixture; set aside until spongy and soft.

3. Measure 1½ cups Strawberry Juice into a small saucepan and bring to a simmer; pour over gelatin mixture and stir to dissolve gelatin. Tint to desired color with red food coloring. Place bowl over bowl of ice water and stir occasionally until the mixture is syrupy and just beginning to thicken (do not let it jell); remove from ice water.

4. When mixture is syrupy, pour a ¹⁄₁₆-inch layer over the top of cake. Decorate top with sliced strawberries arranged in concentric circles, if desired. Carefully brush some of the Strawberry Mirror syrup over the sliced strawberries so they are embedded in a very thin layer of it; refrigerate until set. Pour remaining Strawberry Mirror syrup over fruit until just covered; refrigerate until set.

Strawberry Juice Wash and hull strawberries; coarsely chop. Place strawberries in saucepan; crush to start juices flowing. Place over low heat; add sugar and water; simmer slowly 10 minutes. Pour juice and pulp through damp jelly bag or cheesecloth-lined colander and drain into a bowl for 15 minutes. (Do not press down on fruit.)

You may wonder how this stunning Strawberry Mirror Cake could possibly be easy to prepare. It's the perfect do-ahead dessert that can be broken down into four simple recipes. The mirror top makes a spectacular finish for the cake.

A glaze is being applied to this luscious Orange Custard Tart (page 76). The thin slices of candied orange resemble the petals of an opening flower.

Pies & Tarts

What makes a pie a pie and a tart a tart? You might call the tart a French cousin to the pie, for their similarities seem to put them in the same family. They both have a pastry crust and a filling and are usually served in wedges. However, the similarities between pies and tarts fade when we take a closer look at the nature of their crusts, the shape of the pans they are baked in, and the way they are presented and served.

COMPARING PIES AND TARTS

Pies are known for their tender, flaky short crusts and are usually made with lard or shortening. Pie dough is easier to handle than tart pastry, and can be used to form double-crust and lattice-top pies with decoratively fluted edges. Because flaky pie crusts are fragile when baked, they must remain in their pie plate for support. A pie is baked in a 2-inch-deep pie plate or tin with a slanted, rimmed side and is served directly from the pie plate.

A tart has a sweet short crust made with butter and eggs. These ingredients make the pastry rich and crumbly rather than flaky. A tart is baked in a shallow, rimless, straight-sided tart tin with a removable bottom, or in a tart band positioned on a baking sheet. When baked, the once-fragile pastry develops enough strength to form a pastry shell that can support its filling without the help of the tart tin. After baking, the sides of the tart tin are slipped off to reveal a freestanding pastry that can be presented on a serving platter.

Perhaps the greatest difference between pies and tarts is in the way they are presented and served. American pies are known for their homespun, rustic charm. They are traditionally served in thick slices with a scoop of ice cream or a generous dollop of whipped cream. Tarts, on the other hand, are often thought of as a pastry chef's creation, elegantly adorned with fancy glazes and delicate rosettes of Chantilly Cream.

There is some truth in this lore, but neither pies nor tarts need be held to their reputations! Tarts can be simple country fare eaten in hand-held wedges at a picnic. A pie can be as delicately fashioned and beautifully served as the most elegant of French tarts. Such a wedge of pie can be served anywhere!

ABOUT FLAKY PIE CRUSTS

We remember delicious homemade pies for their flaky, tender crusts as much as for their luscious fillings. The secret of a perfect crust seems to elude many pie bakers. Have you ever asked someone, "Can you give me a good recipe for pie crust?" Every cook will suggest a different addition that they guarantee will produce the flaky crust you seek. By now you are tired of hearing about that teaspoon of vinegar or the lump of lard that will be the salvation of your pie crust.

You will be pleased to discover that it takes more than a recipe and that there is not one perfect recipe! There are several recipes that can be perfect if the cook understands the ingredients and knows how to combine them and how to handle the resulting dough.

When making Flaky Pastry or Egg Pastry, pages 56 and 57, follow these tips and the step-by-step instructions for each recipe. Careful measuring, mixing, and handling will help you to make perfect pies every time.

Tips for a Flaky Pie Crust

The three main ingredients in Flaky Pastry are:
1. Flour
2. Fat
3. Liquid

For this basic, all-purpose dough, the flour and fat are cut together (blended) and then moistened to form a dough. Salt is usually added to improve the flavor and color of the baked crust.

Flour Measure flour before sifting. Use all-purpose flour or white pastry flour (unbleached is best). All-purpose flour is a blend of hard (high-gluten) and soft (low-gluten) white wheat flours. Gluten is an elastic protein in wheat that is activated when flour is combined with a liquid and agitated by stirring or kneading. Gluten provides an elastic framework within your dough that holds it together and allows it to stretch and be rolled out without breaking. If the flour contains too much gluten (is too hard) or if you overactivate the gluten by over-working the dough, you will have a tough, misshapen pie crust. Pastry flour (not to be confused with cake flour) is a soft (low-gluten) flour that can be used in place of all-purpose flour. However, it is often difficult to find a source for pastry flour. Ask your local bakery where to get it or ask your grocer to order some.

Fat Use chilled fat (solid vegetable shortening, lard, butter, or some combination of fats). When using more than one type of fat in a recipe (shortening and butter, for example), soften the fats, mix them together, and then chill this mixture. When making pastry in a food processor, measure and freeze the fat before cutting it into the flour. Lard has more shortening power than other fats, so use 1 tablespoon less lard for every $1/3$ cup fat in the recipe.

Since shortening and lard have more shortening power than butter, they produce flakier, more tender crusts. Butter produces a crust that is less tender and flaky, with a rich, buttery flavor and aroma. You can produce a good pie crust by using all shortening, all lard, all butter, or some combination of these fats in any of the basic pie crust recipes in this chapter. Remember the effect the type of fat will have on the crust.

PIE CRUST TEXTURES

Type of Fat	Characteristics of Resulting Pie Crust
All lard	Most tender, most flaky
All vegetable shortening	Next most tender and flaky
Combination of butter and shortening or butter and lard	Somewhat tender and flaky, with buttery aroma and taste
All butter	Least tender and flaky; rich, buttery flavor and aroma

Use the chart above as a guide in producing the type of pie crust you like the most. The pie crusts are listed in order from the most tender and flaky (all lard) to the least tender and flaky (all butter).

For the flakiest crust, cut half of the fat into the flour until it resembles coarse meal. Then cut in the rest of the fat until it resembles small peas. Cut fats in quickly; overmixing results in oily pastry.

Liquid Use ice water or ice-cold liquids. Moisten the fat-coated flour particles by sprinkling the liquid over them and tossing quickly and lightly with a fork. Do not overmix. The resulting crumbly mixture should be neither wet nor dry but just moist enough to be gathered into a ball. Overmixing or overhandling results in a tough crust that will have a tendency to shrink when baked. Too much liquid also contributes to toughness in the baked crust. It is always better to begin by adding the smaller amount of liquid suggested in the recipe. If more liquid is needed, add a few drops or 1 tablespoon at a time until the desired consistency is reached.

Equipment It is entirely possible to make a pie crust with your fingertips and to roll it out on the deck of a ship with a wine bottle. Fortunately we aren't in that predicament every day and can equip our kitchen with:

☐ A pastry blender, a mixer with a paddle attachment, or a food processor with a metal blade.

☐ A clean, straight, smooth rolling pin (wood or marble, with or without handles). Never wash wooden rolling pins. To clean, rub a little flour on rolling pin and wipe with a soft cloth.

☐ A sharp knife and other cutters, and a fluted pastry-cutting wheel.

☐ A ruler.

☐ A heat-resistant glass pie plate or darkened aluminum pie plate (shiny aluminum pie plates should not be used because they reflect heat and produce soggy, undercooked crusts).

☐ Aluminum foil and pie weights (dried beans or metal pie weights).

☐ Some people like to use a cloth rolling pin sleeve and pastry cloth to roll dough on. The same results can be achieved by keeping the work surface and rolling pin lightly floured at all times when rolling out pastry.

See page 9 for more information on baking equipment.

FREEZING SHORT-CRUST DOUGHS

1. Raw dough may be frozen for six to eight weeks. Wrap well with plastic wrap and aluminum foil, date, and freeze. Thaw dough, wrapped, in refrigerator before rolling out.

2. Raw pie or tart shells may be frozen in pans for six to eight weeks. Wrap well with plastic wrap and aluminum foil, date, and freeze. Blind-bake without defrosting or fill and bake according to recipe. It is not necessary to thaw before baking. If you wish to freeze unbaked filled pies, increase the cornstarch by 1 tablespoon. Do not cut vents in top crust. Wrap and freeze up to three months. Bake, unthawed, at 425° F for 15 minutes, then at 375° F for 25 to 35 minutes. Pastry shells and filling may also be frozen separately.

3. You can freeze fully baked pie or tart shells for up to three months. Wrap well, date, and freeze. Loosen wrapping and thaw at room temperature. Crisp unfilled crust at 350° F for 5 to 10 minutes; cool and fill.

4. Baked and filled double-crust fruit pies may be frozen for up to six months. Wrap well, date, and freeze. Loosen wrapping and thaw at room temperature. Warm thawed filled pies in 350° F oven for 10 to 15 minutes (cover edges of crust with aluminum foil to prevent burning).

Flour and shortening have been cut together in a bowl with a pastry blender. Ice water is waiting to be measured and added to complete the dough. In the background a glass pie plate holds an unbaked pastry crust finished with a rope edge.

BASIC PIE CRUST RECIPES

Both Flaky Pastry and Egg Pastry produce tender, flaky pie crusts and are appropriate for most single-crust, double-crust, or lattice-top pies. Flaky Pastry yields the flakiest crust, but Egg Pastry tastes buttery and the dough can be handled more easily.

FLAKY PASTRY

**Single Crust
(for 9- to 10-inch pie)**

1¼ cups flour
¼ teaspoon salt
½ cup cold shortening
3 tablespoons ice water

**Double Crust
(for 9- to 10-inch double-
crust pie or two 9-inch
single-crust pies)**

2¼ cups flour
½ teaspoon salt
¾ cup cold shortening
5 to 7 tablespoons ice water

1. Sift flour and salt together; place in a medium bowl.

2. Divide shortening in half. Cut half of shortening into the flour with fingertips, a pastry blender, two knives, or the paddle attachment of an electric mixer until the mixture resembles coarse meal. (For food processor method, see below.) Then cut in the remaining shortening until the mixture resembles small peas.

3. Sprinkle ice water over the mixture; toss with a fork to moisten dough evenly. Use as few strokes as possible and the minimum amount of water needed. Gently press dough into a ball. (For a double crust, divide dough into two portions and form two balls.) Flatten ball slightly with a few strokes with the side of your hand. Wrap dough in plastic wrap; refrigerate at least 1 hour. Will keep for 2 to 3 days in refrigerator or 1 month in freezer.

To roll out dough, see "Rolling Out Pastry Dough," page 58.

Flaky Pastry in a Food Processor Measure shortening; freeze until firm. Place flour and salt in bowl of processor fitted with metal blade. Add half of the frozen shortening (cut into small pieces). Process with half-second pulses until the mixture resembles coarse meal. Add remaining shortening; process with half-second pulses until mixture resembles small peas. Add ice water quickly through feed tube with motor running; immediately turn off motor. Mixture should look crumbly but not dry. (Add more ice water, 1 tablespoon at a time, as necessary to moisten dough.) Gather dough into a ball, flatten slightly, wrap, and refrigerate at least 1 hour.

EGG PASTRY

This pastry crust, made with butter and egg yolks, is easier to work with and can take more handling than flaky pastry. The butter and egg yolks lend a rich golden hue to the crust and improve the flavor. A little vinegar or lemon juice helps to soften the gluten and produce a tender crust. Egg Pastry is flaky but somewhat sturdier than Flaky Pastry, so it's especially well suited for pies and tarts with moist custard fillings, for rich pies, and for certain freestanding deep-dish tarts. If you prefer, you can use all butter in this recipe.

Single Crust (for 9- to 10-inch pie)

- 1¼ cups flour
- ½ teaspoon sugar
- ¼ teaspoon salt
- ¼ cup each *unsalted butter and vegetable shortening, combined and chilled*
- ½ teaspoon vinegar
- 1 egg yolk
- 2 to 3 tablespoons ice water

Deep-Dish Tart (for 9- to 10-inch pie)

- 1½ cups flour
- ½ teaspoon sugar
- ¼ teaspoon salt
- ⅓ cup *unsalted butter* and 3 tablespoons *vegetable shortening, combined and chilled*
- ½ teaspoon vinegar
- 1 *extra-large egg yolk*
- 3 to 5 tablespoons ice water

Double Crust (for 9- to 10-inch pie)

- 2¼ cups flour
- 1 teaspoon sugar
- ½ teaspoon salt
- ½ cup *unsalted butter* and ¼ cup *vegetable shortening, combined and chilled*
- 1 teaspoon vinegar
- 2 *large egg yolks*
- 4 to 6 tablespoons ice water

1. Place flour, sugar, and salt in a medium bowl. Cut cold butter/shortening mixture into pieces and add to flour. Cut into flour with fingertips, a pastry blender, 2 knives, or paddle attachment on electric mixer until mixture resembles coarse meal. (For food processor method, see below.)

2. Mix vinegar and egg yolk with smaller amount of ice water in a small bowl. Sprinkle liquid mixture over flour and toss with a fork to moisten dough evenly. Use as few strokes as possible and the minimum amount of water needed to moisten ingredients enough to gather dough into a ball. Add more water, 1 tablespoon at a time, if dough is too dry. Gently press dough into a ball; flatten ball with side of hand. (For a double crust, divide dough into two portions and form two balls.) Wrap dough with plastic wrap; refrigerate at least 1 hour. Will keep for 2 to 3 days in refrigerator or 1 month in freezer.

To roll out dough, see "Rolling Out Pastry Dough," page 58.

Egg Pastry in a Food Processor

Mix butter and shortening together; freeze. Place flour, sugar, and salt in bowl of food processor with metal blade. Cut frozen butter/shortening mixture into pieces and add to bowl; process with half-second pulses until mixture resembles coarse meal. Combine vinegar, egg yolk, and smaller amount of ice water in a bowl; add liquids quickly through feed tube with motor running; stop motor immediately. Mixture should look crumbly but not dry. (Add more water, 1 tablespoon at a time, if necessary to moisten dough.) Gather dough into a ball; flatten slightly with side of hand; wrap and refrigerate for at least 1 hour.

Nut Egg Pastry Use Egg Pastry recipe. Substitute ¼ cup finely ground nuts for ¼ cup of the flour. Ground almonds, pecans, hazelnuts, or walnuts can be used. For a sweeter crust, add 3 tablespoons sifted confectioners' sugar to the flour. This crust is less flaky and tender than regular Egg Pastry, but the nutty flavor is delicious. Finely grated orange or lemon rind can be added if desired. Follow method at left for making Egg Pastry.

LEMON SABLÉE PASTRY

More fragile than most pie crusts, this one can be used for any kind of lemon pie or tart, and some berry pastries also. If you have extra dough, make it into cookies, following the instructions for Orange Sand Cookies, page 119.

- ⅔ cup *finely ground blanched almonds (almond meal)*
- ⅔ cup *sifted confectioners' sugar*
- 11 tablespoons *unsalted butter, at room temperature*
- 1 *egg*
- 2 teaspoons *finely grated lemon rind*
- ⅛ teaspoon *salt*
- 1⅔ cups *flour*

1. Whirl almond meal and sugar in food processor until it becomes a fine powder, about 10 seconds. Transfer to the small bowl of an electric mixer.

2. Add butter to almond-sugar mixture and beat until light. Blend in egg, lemon rind, and salt. Add flour all at once and mix until just combined. Do not overmix.

3. Gather dough in a ball. Wrap and refrigerate 3 hours or until firm enough to roll out.

To roll out dough, see "Rolling Out Pastry Dough," page 58.

Makes one 9- to 10-inch pastry crust.

ROLLING OUT PASTRY DOUGH

Remove dough from refrigerator and allow to soften slightly before rolling. Place dough on lightly floured surface. Sprinkle a little flour on top of dough or rub some flour on the rolling pin. Roll dough from the center toward the edges (easing pressure on the rolling pin near edge of dough) to form a circle of dough ⅛ inch thick, large enough to extend 2 inches beyond the rim of the pie plate. Lift dough and give a quarter turn after each rolling, re-flouring surfaces as necessary to prevent sticking and tearing. Cupping hands slightly, reshape dough into a circle. If dough cracks or tears, brush the tear with water and apply a thin piece of dough to patch it. (It is better to patch dough than to reroll it because rerolling will toughen it.)

To transfer dough to pie plate, place rolling pin just to one side of the center of the dough. Lightly drape half of dough over the rolling pin, rest dough across pie plate, and unfold dough onto pie plate. Fit dough into plate with fingertips or a small ball of dough.

For a Single Crust Trim edge so it extends ½ inch to 1 inch beyond edge of pie plate. Fold edges of dough under. Finish edges (see page 59). Blind-bake (see page 60) or fill and bake.

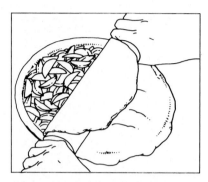

For a Double Crust Trim lower crust even with rim of pie plate. Roll out second piece of dough (for top) slightly thinner than bottom crust. Fill pie; brush rim of bottom crust with cold water. Place top crust on pie; press edges to seal; trim edges to ½ inch from rim and finish edges (see page 59). Cut steam vents (slits or designs) in top crust before or after crust is on pie. Bake according to the directions in individual recipes.

Decorating Double-Crust Pies

Decorating the top crust with pastry cutouts is fun and lends a festive touch to your pie. Roll out scraps of dough as thin as possible and use cookie cutters or a knife to cut out different shapes to apply to the top (stems, leaves, flowers, stars, fruits, and so forth). Brush cutouts with water and press into place on top crust.

You may brush the top crust with one of the following glazes: (1) milk and a sprinkling of sugar, (2) cream, or (3) egg or egg yolk lightly beaten with a pinch of salt and 1 teaspoon of water—this adds a shiny golden brown glaze to your pie.

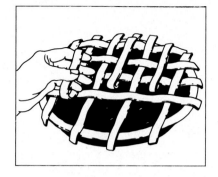

Lattice-Top Pies

Line pie plate with pastry and trim bottom crust to ½ inch beyond rim. Roll out a circle of dough 2 inches larger than rim of pie plate for lattice top. Cut strips of dough ½ inch wide with a knife or fluted pastry-cutting wheel and a ruler. Fill pie. Lay half of the strips of pastry ¾ inch apart across pie. Fold back every other strip at center. Lay a strip across the unfolded strips; unfold other strips over this. Fold back the alternating strips (ones that were lying flat last time) and lay the next strip ¾ inch from the last. Continue until this half of the pie is latticed. Repeat this procedure on other side of pie. Trim lattice strips to match edge of bottom crust; lift lattice strips at edge and moisten rim of crust underneath; press lattice strips onto bottom crust at edge of pie. Flute edges (see page 59). See photo of Strawberry-Rhubarb Pie (page 64) for an example of a lattice top.

PIE CRUST EDGES

To make attractive edges for single- or double-crust pies, allow pastry to extend ½ inch to 1 inch beyond rim of pie plate. Fold edge of dough under so it is even with the edge of the pie plate to create a raised, even rim.

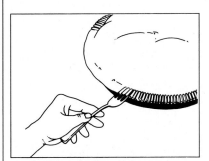

Fork-Fluted Edge *Trim pastry even with rim of pie plate. Firmly press tines of fork into pastry around entire rim of pie plate.*

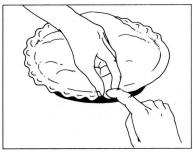

Fluted Edge *Place left index finger on inside of rim, pointing toward outside of shell. Pinch pastry into V shape between right index finger and thumb; repeat along entire edge. Pinch again to sharpen points.*

Rope Edge *Press thumb at an angle into pastry and pinch pastry toward thumb with bent index finger; repeat along entire edge.*

Ruffle Edge *Place left thumb and index finger 1 inch apart on edge of pastry, pointing toward outside of shell. Gently pull pastry between them toward outside of shell with right index finger. Repeat along entire edge.*

Spiral Edge *Trim pastry even with edge of pie plate. Brush rim with water. Cut long, straight ¾-inch strips of pastry. Press one end of strip to rim, twist strip and press into rim with index finger after each twist.*

Braided Edge *Trim pastry even with edge of pie. Brush rim of pastry with water. Cut two long, straight ½-inch strips of pastry. Press end of strips to rim. Interlace strips in a flat braid on top of rim, pressing part of lower strip onto the pastry underneath to secure the braid after each overlap. Try to keep strips flat and avoid stretching pastry.*

CHANTILLY CREAM

Chantilly Cream is a fancy name for sweetened, flavored whipped cream. It is the preferred topping for many hot and cold desserts. It can also be a filling for a pie or cake, and can be used to lighten other creams and fillings. The following recipe can be doubled or tripled easily if you need more than the 1 cup this recipe produces.

> ½ cup whipping cream
> 1 tablespoon sifted confectioners' sugar
> ¼ teaspoon vanilla extract or 1 teaspoon liqueur

1. Chill the cream, mixing bowl, and beaters (or whisk) before whipping the cream.

2. Whip the cream until it begins to thicken; add sugar and vanilla or liqueur. Continue beating until cream holds its shape on the beaters and forms peaks (cream should still look smooth and soft; do not overbeat, or cream will become grainy or turn to butter). Slightly underbeat cream if you will be piping it from a pastry bag fitted with a star tip (the tip whips the cream a little more).

Makes 1 cup.

BLIND-BAKING

Blind-baking is a method used to prebake a pastry crust for a pie or tart before it is filled to create an empty pastry shell. The pastry shell can be either partially baked or fully baked, depending on the way it is to be filled.

Partially Baked Shells Because some custard and cream fillings bake at low oven temperatures or for a short time, the pastry crust underneath will be uncooked and soggy if it is not partially baked before the filling is added. To ensure a crisp bottom crust, we recommend a longer baking time for partially baked crusts than the times indicated in other cookbooks. The crust should be almost done and beginning to color. Cool crust completely; add cool filling to cool crust and return to preheated oven to complete baking. (A hot filling or hot crust can result in a soggy bottom crust because hot filling is more penetrating and hot crust more absorbent.)

1. Preheat oven to 400° F. Cut a circle of aluminum foil or parchment paper 2 inches larger than the diameter of the pie plate. Fit paper into pastry-lined plate and allow it to project 1 inch above the rim. Fill the foil with dried beans to support the sides of the pie or the tart pastry while it bakes.

2. Bake for 10 to 15 minutes or until crust is set. Carefully remove the foil and the beans.

3. Cover edges of crust with strips of foil (to prevent overbrowning) and bake empty pastry shell until crust looks almost done but not fully brown, 5 to 10 minutes longer. Crust will be a very pale color with some areas just beginning to turn golden. Pie crusts bake more quickly than tart crusts, so bake them for the shorter times indicated.

4. Cool completely, then fill and bake as directed in individual recipes.

Fully Baked Pastry Shells Fully baked pastry shells are blind-baked until completely done and golden brown all over. These shells are used to hold an uncooked filling (fresh fruit), a cold filling (mousse, Bavarian cream), or a filling that is cooked on the top of the stove and added later (lemon curd, pudding). Cool fillings are usually added to cooled, fully baked shells.

1. Preheat oven to 400° F. Cut a circle of aluminum foil or parchment paper 2 inches larger than the diameter of the pie plate. Fit paper into pastry-lined plate and allow it to project 1 inch above the rim. Fill the foil with dried beans to support the sides of the pie or tart pastry while it bakes.

2. Bake for 10 to 15 minutes or until crust is set. Carefully remove foil and beans. Prick the pastry crust with a fork to allow steam to escape.

3. Bake empty pastry shell until golden brown, 10 to 15 minutes more. Remember that pie shells bake more quickly than tart shells and should be watched carefully, to avoid burning.

4. Cool completely before filling.

VIRGINIA PEACH PIE

Fresh, ripe peaches are baked in a nut pie crust and topped with buttery almond-pecan crumble. Use almonds or pecans for the crust. For a change of pace, omit the nut topping and bake as a double-crust or lattice-top pie. Serve warm or at room temperature with Chantilly Cream (see page 59) or ice cream.

- 1 9-inch single-crust Nut Egg Pastry (see page 57)
- 5 cups peeled, sliced freestone peaches (5 to 6 large peaches)
- ½ to ¾ cup granulated sugar
- 2½ to 3 tablespoons cornstarch Dash ground nutmeg
- 1 tablespoon lemon juice
- ⅛ teaspoon almond extract
- 1 egg white, lightly beaten (optional)
- ⅓ cup light brown sugar
- ½ cup flour
- 6 tablespoons unsalted butter
- 1 cup chopped nuts (mixture of almonds and pecans)

1. Preheat oven to 425° F. Line a 9-inch pie plate with Nut Egg Pastry. To make the peaches easier to peel, dip them in boiling water, then in cold water. In a large bowl combine sliced peaches, ½ to ¾ cup granulated sugar (depending on ripeness of peaches), cornstarch, and nutmeg. Allow to stand 15 minutes.

2. Stir in lemon juice and almond extract.

3. Lightly brush uncooked pie shell with a thin layer of egg white (if used) to moisture-proof pie crust. Pour filling into pie shell.

4. Mix brown sugar with flour; cut in butter until crumbly. Stir in nuts. Sprinkle mixture over peaches.

5. Bake for 15 minutes. Reduce oven to 400° F and continue baking for 35 to 40 minutes. Cover edges of crust with strips of foil, if necessary, to prevent excessive browning.

Serves 8.

SOUTHERN PECAN PIE

This traditional American pie is a favorite of almost everyone. It is easy to make and just as easy to eat. Serve it topped with vanilla ice cream or whipped cream.

  1 9-inch single-crust Egg Pastry (see page 57)
  4 eggs, lightly beaten
  ⅔ cup dark brown sugar
1⅓ cups light corn syrup
  ¼ cup unsalted butter, melted
  ½ teaspoon salt
  4 teaspoons flour
  2 teaspoons vanilla extract
1¼ cups coarsely chopped pecans

1. Line a 9-inch pie plate with Egg Pastry and blind-bake until partially baked (see page 60).

2. Preheat oven to 375° F. In a large bowl combine eggs, sugar, corn syrup, butter, salt, flour, and vanilla; stir to blend. Stir in pecans. Pour into partially baked pie shell.

3. Bake until custard is set (30 to 40 minutes). Cover edges of crust with strips of foil, if necessary, to prevent excessive browning. Cool on wire rack.

Serves 8.

This Virginia Peach Pie is baked in an almond pie crust and topped with an almond-pecan crumble. It's a perfect dessert for summer, when peaches are in season.

RASPBERRY PIE

Blackberries, olallieberries, or logan-berries can also be used to make this pie. Care must be taken in the preparation of berry pies to produce a perfectly thickened filling in a crisp crust. Select firm, ripe berries, and rinse them quickly (do not soak in water). Since berries vary in tartness, some require more sugar than others.

- 1 9-inch double-crust Flaky Pastry or Egg Pastry (see pages 56-57)
- 5 cups fresh raspberries (5 half-pint baskets)
- 6 tablespoons flour
- ½ cup sugar
- 1 egg white, lightly beaten
- 1 tablespoon unsalted butter (optional)

1. Preheat oven to 425° F. Roll out pastry for bottom crust and line a 9-inch pie plate. Roll out remaining pastry to form the top crust (see page 58).

2. Rinse berries, drain, and dry on paper towels. In a bowl combine berries with flour and sugar.

3. Brush inside of bottom crust with egg white to moisture-proof the crust. Place filling in shell. Dot with butter (if used).

4. Moisten rim of bottom pie crust with water and cover with top crust; seal and finish edges; cut vents in top.

5. Place pie on a rimmed baking sheet and bake for 15 minutes. Reduce oven to 350° F and continue baking until crust is golden brown (40 to 50 minutes). Cover edges of crust with strips of foil, if necessary, to prevent excessive browning. Serve at room temperature.

Serves 8.

SOUR-CHERRY PIE

A lattice-top cherry pie shows off the ripe, red fruit to perfection.

- 1 9-inch double-crust Flaky Pastry or Egg Pastry (see pages 56-57)
- 1¼ cups sugar
- 5 tablespoons flour
- ⅔ cup cherry juice or other red fruit juice
- ½ teaspoon ground cinnamon
- ⅛ teaspoon almond extract
- 1 tablespoon lemon juice
- 5 cups pitted tart red cherries
- 1 egg white, lightly beaten
- 1½ tablespoons unsalted butter

1. Preheat oven to 425° F. Roll out pastry for bottom crust and line a 9-inch pie plate. Roll out remaining pastry to form top crust or lattice top (see page 58).

2. In a saucepan combine sugar, flour, cherry juice, cinnamon, almond extract, lemon juice, and cherries. Cook over low heat, stirring frequently, until mixture thickens; cool.

3. Brush inside of bottom crust with egg white to moisture-proof the crust. Pour in cooled filling. Dot with butter.

4. Moisten edges of bottom crust and cover with top crust or lattice top; finish edges. Bake for 20 minutes. Lower heat to 400° F and continue baking until crust is golden brown (40 minutes). Cover edges of crust with strips of foil, if necessary, to prevent excessive browning.

Serves 8.

APPLE PIE

Tart apples, such as Granny Smiths or pippins, make the best apple pie. Remember to pile the apple slices high in the center because they cook down during baking.

- 1 9-inch double-crust Flaky Pastry or Egg Pastry (see pages 56-57)
- 6 to 8 tart apples, peeled, cored, and thinly sliced (6 cups)
- ¾ cup sugar
- ¾ teaspoon ground cinnamon
- ⅛ teaspoon ground nutmeg
- 2 tablespoons cornstarch
- 2 teaspoons lemon juice
- 1 teaspoon finely grated lemon rind
- 1 egg white, lightly beaten
- 2 tablespoons cold unsalted butter
- 1 egg yolk beaten with 1 teaspoon water

1. Preheat oven to 425° F. Roll out pastry for bottom crust and line a 9-inch pie plate. Roll out remaining pastry for top crust (see page 58).

2. In a large bowl combine apple slices, sugar, cinnamon, nutmeg, and cornstarch; stir. Allow to stand 15 minutes. Stir in lemon juice and lemon rind.

3. Brush inside of bottom crust with egg white to moisture-proof the crust. Arrange apple slices in pie shell in flat, snug layers. Create a higher mound of apple slices in the center. Pour juices from bowl over apples; dot with pieces of butter.

4. Moisten rim of bottom crust and cover with top crust. Seal and finish edges; cut vents in top. Brush with egg yolk beaten with water.

5. Bake for 15 minutes. Lower oven temperature to 400° F; continue baking until crust is golden brown (35 to 40 minutes). For a sugared crust, brush pie again with egg yolk glaze 5 minutes before pie is done; sprinkle with sugar.

Serves 6 to 8.

*The flavor of Apple Pie fresh from
the oven is difficult to surpass.
The top crust is decorated with
heart-shaped pastry cutouts.
Serve this pie with ice cream.*

The tart, refreshing flavor of rhubarb with sweet strawberries makes a delicious pie. The addition of raisins and ginger gives it an unusual twist.

LATTICE-TOP RAISIN PIE

This pie's lingering warmth satisfies robust cold-weather appetites. It's best when served warm with a scoop of vanilla ice cream or a glass of port. If you want to make a whole pie, you'll be happy to know that it keeps for several days at room temperature.

- 1 9-inch double-crust Flaky Pastry or Egg Pastry (see pages 56–57)
- 1¾ cups water
- 2 cups seedless raisins
- ½ teaspoon finely grated lemon rind
- 1 teaspoon finely grated orange rind
- ½ cup light brown sugar
- 2 tablespoons flour
- ⅛ teaspoon salt
- ½ teaspoon ground cinnamon
- ¼ cup orange juice
- 2 tablespoons lemon juice
- 1 tablespoon unsalted butter
- 2 teaspoons brandy or Cognac (optional)
- ½ cup chopped pecans or walnuts, lightly toasted
- 2 tablespoons milk (optional)
- 2 tablespoons granulated sugar (optional)

1. Preheat oven to 400° F. Roll out pastry for bottom crust and line a 9-inch pie plate. Roll out remaining pastry to form lattice top.

2. In a saucepan combine water, raisins, and lemon and orange rind. Bring to a boil; boil 5 minutes. Stir in brown sugar. Remove from heat.

3. In a small bowl combine flour, salt, cinnamon, and orange juice; stir until flour dissolves. Add to saucepan with raisins; cook over medium heat, stirring constantly, until mixture thickens.

4. Remove from heat; stir in lemon juice, butter, brandy (if used), and pecans. Cool to room temperature.

5. Fill pie shell. Moisten edges of bottom crust; attach lattice top; seal and finish edges. Brush with milk and sprinkle with the 2 tablespoons granulated sugar, if desired. Bake until crust is golden brown (35 to 40 minutes). Cover edges of crust with strips of foil, if necessary, to prevent excessive browning.

Serves 8 to 10.

STRAWBERRY-RHUBARB PIE

For a delicious taste treat, add raisins and ginger to Strawberry-Rhubarb Pie. Serve it when freshly baked with vanilla ice cream, or refrigerate it and discover how refreshing it can be when served ice cold on a hot summer day.

- 1 9-inch double-crust Flaky Pastry or Egg Pastry (see pages 56–57)
- 2 cups washed, hulled, and halved strawberries (one 12-oz basket)
- 4 cups young, unpeeled rhubarb stalks, sliced
- ⅓ cup seedless raisins
- 1⅓ cups sugar
- 6 tablespoons flour
- ¼ teaspoon ground ginger
- 1 egg white, lightly beaten
- 1½ tablespoons unsalted butter

1. Preheat oven to 425° F. Roll out pastry for bottom crust and line a 9-inch pie plate. Roll out remaining pastry to form top crust or lattice top (see page 58).

2. In a large bowl combine strawberries, rhubarb, raisins, sugar, flour, and ginger; let stand 15 minutes.

3. Brush inside of bottom crust with egg white to moisture-proof. Pour filling into shell. Dot with butter.

4. Moisten rim of bottom crust with water and cover with top crust or lattice top; seal and finish edges.

5. Place pie on a rimmed baking sheet and bake for 20 minutes. Lower oven to 400° F and continue baking until crust is golden brown (40 minutes). Cover edges of crust with strips of foil, if necessary, to prevent excessive browning.

Serves 8.

LEMON MERINGUE PIE

This version of lemon pie filling derives its rich yellow hue from egg yolks, butter, and lemon zest—no yellow food coloring here! The quick and easy lemon curd filling can be poured piping hot directly into a fully baked shell. Almonds are a good choice if you make a nut crust.

- 1 9-inch single-crust Flaky Pastry, Egg Pastry, or Nut Egg Pastry (see pages 56–57)
- 4 whole eggs
- 3 egg yolks (reserve whites for Meringue Topping)
- 1 cup plus 2 tablespoons sugar
- ¾ cup lemon juice
- 2 teaspoons finely grated lemon rind
- 9 tablespoons unsalted butter, softened
  Meringue Topping (see page 66)

1. Line a 9-inch pie plate with pastry and blind-bake until fully baked (see page 60); cool.

2. In a stainless steel bowl, combine eggs, egg yolks, sugar, lemon juice, and lemon rind. Place bowl over a pot of boiling water and whisk or stir over medium heat until mixture thickens to the consistency of mayonnaise, about 5 minutes. Do not boil or eggs will curdle!

3. Remove from heat; whisk in soft butter, 2 tablespoons at a time, until all butter is incorporated. Pour immediately into fully baked pie shell. Cool to room temperature before topping with meringue.

4. Preheat oven to 350° F. Prepare Meringue Topping. Spread meringue over surface of pie, sealing meringue to edges of crust all around. Bake until golden brown (10 to 15 minutes). Serve at room temperature.

Serves 6 to 8.

HOW TO OPEN A COCONUT

Force an ice pick through each of the dark depressions (eyes) at one end of the coconut, and drain off the liquid.

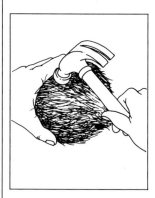

Freeze the coconut for 1 hour. Remove from freezer and break open the shell by tapping sharply with a hammer or by throwing it onto cement. Meat will separate easily from skin. Pare off any brown skin remaining on the white meat. Store coconut, well wrapped, in refrigerator. It will keep for at least a week. Shred when ready to use. Large holes on grater will produce flaked coconut; smaller holes produce narrow shreds. Half of a small (1 lb) coconut is plenty for this pie.

COCONUT CREAM PIE

This velvety coconut cream filling is absolutely delicious made with either freshly grated coconut or dried, flaked coconut.

In the Hawaiian islands, locals deftly split open coconuts with giant razor-sharp machetes. Here, where machetes are more scarce than fresh coconuts, we must resort to other means of opening the rock-hard shells. Hammering your coconut or throwing it on cement (as described at left) is nearly as entertaining as the machete method and is actually a more effective way to separate the meat from the shell.

> 1 9-inch single-crust Flaky Pastry, Egg Pastry (see pages 56–57), or Coconut-Flake Crust (below)
> ½ cup sugar
> 2 tablespoons cornstarch
> 3 tablespoons flour
> 2½ cups milk
> 3 egg yolks (reserve whites for Meringue Topping)
> 1 teaspoon vanilla extract
> 2 tablespoons unsalted butter
> 1 cup flaked fresh coconut or 1½ cups dried flaked coconut

Coconut-Flake Crust

> 3 tablespoons unsalted butter, softened
> 1½ to 2 cups flaked coconut

Meringue Topping

> 3 egg whites, at room temperature
> ¼ teaspoon cream of tartar
> ¼ teaspoon cornstarch
> 4 tablespoons superfine sugar
> ½ teaspoon vanilla extract
> ¼ cup flaked coconut

1. Line a 9-inch pie plate with pastry and blind-bake until fully baked (see page 60) or prepare Coconut-Flake Crust.

2. In a saucepan combine sugar, cornstarch, and flour; stir in milk. Cook over medium heat until thick and bubbly, stirring constantly, then cook 2 minutes longer. Remove from heat and stir about ½ cup of hot mixture into egg yolks. Stir warmed yolks into hot mixture and cook over medium heat, stirring constantly, until thick, about 2 minutes.

3. Remove from heat, stir in vanilla, butter, and coconut. Cool to room temperature. Prepare Meringue Topping.

4. Preheat oven to 350° F. Fill pie shell with cooled coconut cream. Spread Meringue Topping on top of pie and bake. Cool before serving. Store pie in refrigerator if it won't be served within an hour after baking. The filling will firm to a nice cutting consistency when chilled. Pie can be served with Chantilly Cream (see page 59) instead of meringue.

Serves 6 to 8.

Coconut-Flake Crust Preheat oven to 325° F. Spread soft butter evenly inside a 9-inch pie plate. Distribute flaked coconut in an even layer over butter. Press coconut into butter. Bake until golden brown, about 15 minutes.

Meringue Topping Beat egg whites until foamy. Add cream of tartar and cornstarch. Beat until whites form soft peaks. Add superfine sugar, 1 tablespoon at a time, beating after each addition. Beat in vanilla and continue beating until stiff, glossy peaks form. Spread meringue over the filling, sealing to edge of pastry. Sprinkle flaked coconut over top of meringue. Bake at 350° F until golden brown (10 to 15 minutes). To cut meringue easily, dip the knife into water.

CRUMB CRUSTS

Crumb crusts are just right for the chilled or frozen fillings of do-ahead Bavarian cream, chiffon, or ice cream pies, and best of all they're easy to prepare—just add a little sugar to the crumbs and stir in butter. Press crumb crust mixture into the pie plate, chill, and fill. There's no dough to roll or bake—an attractive feature during warm weather!

These crusts can be made in as many flavors as there are dry crumbs. Some cookie or cracker crumbs that are commonly used for crumb crusts are: vanilla wafers, chocolate wafers, gingersnaps, dry macaroons, Amaretti cookies, graham crackers, and zwieback or melba toast. Cookie crumbs usually do not require the addition of sugar. Cracker and toast crumbs will need to be sweetened. Finely ground nuts, poppy seed, or sesame seed can be substituted for some of the crumbs for variety.

CRUMB CRUST

> 2 cups fine crumbs (see step 1)
> ¼ cup sifted confectioners' sugar
> ½ cup unsalted butter, melted
> Ground cinnamon or nutmeg (optional)

1. Break crackers, cookies, cake, or bread into small pieces. Grind a small amount at a time in a food processor or electric blender. Place fine crumbs in a bowl.

2. Stir sugar, butter, and cinnamon (if used) into crumbs (see Note). (Taste crumbs before adding sugar or cinnamon—they may already be sweet and spicy.)

3. Spread crumb mixture evenly over bottom and sides of a well-buttered 9-inch pie plate. Press an 8-inch pie plate onto the crumb mixture to pack down and evenly distribute the crumbs in the plate. Nicely shape crumbs on rim of pie plate and press to mold rim.

4. To set crust, refrigerate for 30 minutes *or* bake in a preheated 325° F oven for 10 minutes (cool before filling). Fill as directed in recipe.

Note For a baked crumb crust that doesn't crumble, add one lightly beaten egg white to crumb mixture; bake as directed above.

Chocolate Crumb Crust Either (1) use chocolate wafer crumbs in the Crumb Crust recipe, or (2) melt 2 ounces semisweet chocolate with the butter in the Crumb Crust recipe.

PRESS-IN NUT CRUST

This crust has no crumbs, just nuts. Fill with any of the Bavarian cream or mousse pie fillings.

> 1½ cups finely ground nuts (almonds, hazelnuts, pecans or walnuts)
> ¼ cup sifted confectioners' sugar
> ¼ cup unsalted butter, melted
> 1 egg white, lightly beaten

1. Preheat oven to 350° F. Combine nuts and sugar in a bowl; stir in melted butter. Add egg white and mix well.

2. Spread nut mixture evenly over bottom, sides, and rim of a well-buttered 9-inch pie plate. Press an 8-inch pie plate into the nut mixture to pack down and evenly distribute nuts in the plate. Shape and flute the edges.

3. Bake until crust is set (10 to 15 minutes). Cover edges of crust with strips of foil, if necessary, to prevent excessive browning. Cool and fill as directed in recipe.

Chocolate Press-In Nut Crust

Melt 2 ounces semisweet chocolate with butter in Press-In Nut Crust recipe, above.

HOW TO PEEL AND GRIND NUTS

Almonds: To blanch almonds, drop shelled nuts into boiling water for one minute; rinse in cold water; drain. Pinch each nut to slip skin off. To dry, spread on baking sheet and heat in 350° F oven for 5 minutes or dry at room temperature for 2 days.

Pistachio nuts: Drop nuts in boiling water for one minute; rinse in cold water; drain. Remove skins with your fingers and a small sharp knife (if necessary). To dry, see Almonds.

Hazelnuts (also called filberts): Preheat oven to 350° F. Spread nuts in a single layer on a baking sheet. Heat for 7 minutes to loosen skins. Remove from oven; rub nuts against a fine-mesh wire sieve or a metal colander to remove skins.

Pecans and Walnuts: Do not need to be skinned.

To Grind Nuts

In a food processor fitted with the metal blade or in a blender, place nuts and blend in short bursts (1-second pulses) until nuts are ground to a fine meal. Check the nuts frequently to avoid bringing out the oil or producing a paste. If possible, grind the nuts with some of the sugar or flour in the recipe.

*Mocha Bavarian Pie features a
chocolate crumb crust. Chantilly
Cream is piped around the
pie's edge. Candied coffee beans
are the finishing touch.*

EGGNOG PIE

Imagine eggnog so thick and creamy you can eat it with a fork!

- 1 tablespoon unflavored gelatin (1 envelope)
- ¼ cup cold water
- 4 egg yolks
- ⅓ cup sugar
- 1⅓ cups milk
- ¾ cup whipping cream
- ¼ teaspoon ground nutmeg
- ¼ cup dark rum
- 1 cup Chantilly Cream (see page 59)

Almond Crumb Crust

- ¾ cup finely ground almonds
- 1¼ cups fine graham cracker crumbs
- 2 tablespoons sifted confectioners' sugar
- ¼ teaspoon ground nutmeg
- ½ cup butter, melted

1. Prepare Almond Crumb Crust mixture. Reserve ¼ cup crumb mixture to decorate top of pie. Press remaining mixture into bottom and up sides of a well-buttered 9-inch pie plate. Refrigerate or bake (see Crumb Crust, page 67).

2. Sprinkle gelatin over cold water; set aside until soft and spongy.

3. Beat egg yolks and sugar together until thick and light-colored.

4. Bring milk to a boil in a saucepan. Pour hot milk into yolk mixture; stir to blend. Return to saucepan; cook over low heat, stirring constantly with a wooden spoon, until custard thickens slightly, and your finger leaves a clear trail when drawn across the back of a wooden spoon. This is a thin custard about the consistency of unwhipped whipping cream. Note: You may cook over a double boiler to lessen the risk of curdling the yolks.

5. Whisk softened gelatin into the hot custard; transfer to a medium bowl. Place bowl over ice water, stirring frequently, until mixture thickens to the consistency of softly whipped cream.

6. While custard is thickening, whip whipping cream until it holds soft peaks; refrigerate.

7. When custard mixture is the consistency of softly whipped cream, stir in nutmeg and rum, then fold in whipped cream. Pour immediately into prepared crust. Refrigerate 2 hours or until filling is firm. To serve, decorate pie with Chantilly Cream and reserved crumbs.

Serves 8.

Almond Crumb Crust Combine ground almonds, graham cracker crumbs, confectioners' sugar, and nutmeg in a bowl. Stir in butter.

MOCHA BAVARIAN PIE

Freshly brewed coffee and dark chocolate blend to produce this mocha cream pie.

- 1 9-inch Chocolate Crumb Crust (see page 67) or Chocolate Press-In Nut Crust (see page 67)
- 4 teaspoons unflavored gelatin (1⅓ envelopes)
- ⅓ cup cold coffee (or water)
- 3 egg yolks
- ½ cup sugar (¾ cup if using espresso)
- 1¼ cups strong, freshly brewed hot coffee
- 2 ounces semisweet chocolate, grated or cut in very small pieces
- 1 cup whipping cream
- 2 egg whites
- 2 tablespoons sugar
- 1 tablespoon coffee-flavored liqueur
- 1½ cups Chantilly Cream (see page 59)
- 2 to 4 ounces semisweet chocolate (for Chocolate Curls, optional)

1. Prepare crust; reserve ¼ cup crumbs from crust for topping, if you wish to decorate with crumbs rather than Chocolate Curls. Sprinkle gelatin over the ⅓ cup cold coffee in a bowl; set aside until soft and spongy.

2. Beat egg yolks and the ½ cup sugar until thick and light-colored.

3. Stir the 1¼ cups hot coffee into yolk mixture; transfer to a saucepan. Stir in the 2 ounces grated chocolate. Cook over low heat, stirring constantly with a wooden spoon, until the custard thickens slightly (do not boil), and your finger leaves a clear trail when drawn across the back of a wooden spoon. This is a thin custard about the consistency of unwhipped heavy cream. Note: You may cook over a double boiler to lessen the risk of curdling the yolks.

4. Stir softened gelatin into hot coffee mixture; transfer to a medium bowl. Place bowl over ice water, stirring frequently, until mixture thickens to the consistency of whipped cream.

5. While custard is thickening, whip whipping cream until it forms soft peaks; refrigerate.

6. Wait to whip the egg whites until just before the coffee mixture reaches the right consistency. Whip the whites until they just begin to hold peaks; beat in the 2 tablespoons sugar, 1 tablespoon at a time. Beat until whites form stiff peaks but are still glossy and smooth.

7. When coffee mixture is the consistency of softly whipped cream, stir in the coffee liqueur; fold in the cream, then fold in the egg whites. These steps should be accomplished quickly to prevent the mixture from setting too rapidly.

8. Pour mixture into prepared crust; refrigerate 2 hours or until filling is firm. Decorate pie with Chantilly Cream; top with reserved crumbs or Chocolate Curls. (See page 33 for instructions on how to make Chocolate Curls.)

Serves 8 to 10.

PUMPKIN-GINGER PIE

This pumpkin pie gives tradition a twist with its light pumpkin chiffon filling and crunchy gingersnap pecan crust.

- 1 tablespoon unflavored gelatin (1 envelope)
- ¼ cup cold water
- ½ cup milk
- ½ teaspoon finely grated orange rind
- 2 egg yolks
- ⅓ cup dark brown sugar
- 1 cup cooked pumpkin purée
- ½ teaspoon ground cinnamon
- ¼ teaspoon ground ginger
- ¼ teaspoon ground nutmeg
- ½ cup whipping cream
- 2 egg whites
- 2 tablespoons granulated sugar
- 1½ cups Chantilly Cream (see page 59)

Gingersnap-Pecan Crumb Crust

- 1¼ cups fine gingersnap crumbs (thirty 1½-inch cookies)
- ¾ cup finely ground pecans (3 oz)
- ¼ cup sifted confectioners' sugar
- ½ cup unsalted butter, melted

1. Prepare Gingersnap-Pecan Crumb Crust mixture. Press into bottom and up sides of a well-buttered 9-inch pie plate. Refrigerate or bake (see Crumb Crust, page 67).

2. Sprinkle gelatin over the water in a small bowl; set aside until gelatin is soft and spongy.

3. Place milk and orange rind in a saucepan; bring to a simmer. Remove from heat, cover, and allow rind to steep in milk for 5 minutes.

4. Beat egg yolks with brown sugar in a medium bowl until light-colored. Reheat the milk to boiling; pour hot milk into yolk mixture, and stir to blend. Return to saucepan; cook over low heat, stirring constantly with a wooden spoon, until custard thickens slightly (do not boil), and your finger leaves a clear trail when drawn across the back of a wooden spoon. This is a thin custard about the consistency of unwhipped whipping cream. Note: You may cook over a double-boiler to lessen the risk of curdling the yolks.

5. Immediately whisk softened gelatin into hot mixture; mix well. Transfer to a medium stainless steel bowl. Stir in pumpkin, cinnamon, ginger, and nutmeg. Place bowl over ice water, stirring frequently, until mixture thickens to the consistency of softly whipped cream.

6. Whip whipping cream until it holds soft peaks; refrigerate.

7. When pumpkin mixture is the consistency of softly whipped cream, remove from ice water and fold in whipped cream. (When pumpkin mixture and cream are the same consistency, they will blend easily to form a smooth Bavarian cream.)

8. Beat egg whites until they form soft peaks. Add sugar, 1 tablespoon at a time, and beat until whites are just stiff but still glossy and smooth (do not overbeat). Fold whites into pumpkin mixture. Pour into prepared crust. Refrigerate until set. Decorate with Chantilly Cream before serving.

Serves 8 to 10.

Gingersnap-Pecan Crumb Crust

Combine gingersnap crumbs, ground pecans, and confectioners' sugar in a bowl. Stir in melted butter. Refrigerate or bake (see Crumb Crust, page 67).

RASPBERRY MOUSSE PIE

Toasted hazelnuts (sometimes called filberts) form the crust for this airy raspberry mousse pie. Top with rosettes of Chantilly Cream and fresh raspberries. To create a chocolate crust, just substitute chocolate wafers for vanilla.

- 1 to 1¼ cups raspberry purée (2 half-pint baskets)
- 2 tablespoons cold water
- 2 tablespoons lemon juice
- 1 tablespoon unflavored gelatin (1 envelope)
- 3 whole eggs
- 2 egg yolks
- ¾ cup sugar (scant)
- 1 tablespoon kirsch
- ¾ cup whipping cream
- 1½ cups Chantilly Cream (see page 59)
  Whole raspberries, for decoration

Hazelnut Crumb Crust

- ¾ cup hazelnuts
- 1¼ cups fine vanilla-wafer crumbs
- ¼ cup sifted confectioners' sugar
- ½ cup butter, melted

1. Prepare Hazelnut Crumb Crust mixture; press into bottom and up sides of a well-buttered 9-inch pie plate. Refrigerate or bake (see Crumb Crust, page 67).

2. Strain raspberry purée to remove seeds (frozen raspberries may be used).

3. Combine cold water and lemon juice in a small bowl; sprinkle gelatin over this mixture; set aside until soft and spongy.

4. In a medium stainless steel bowl, combine eggs, egg yolks, and sugar; place bowl over a pot of hot water and cook, whisking constantly, until your finger leaves a clear trail when drawn across the back of a wooden spoon.

5. Remove from heat, whisk in softened gelatin mixture, and continue beating until cool (this can be done with whip attachment on electric mixer). Stir in raspberry purée and kirsch.

6. Place bowl over ice water, stirring frequently, until mixture thickens to the consistency of softly whipped cream. Meanwhile, whip whipping cream until it begins to form soft peaks. When raspberry mixture is the right consistency, fold whipped cream into it. Immediately pour into prepared crumb crust. Refrigerate 2 hours or until firm. Decorate with Chantilly Cream and whole raspberries before serving. *Serves 8 to 10.*

Hazelnut Crumb Crust Skin and finely grind hazelnuts (see page 67). Combine ground hazelnuts, fine vanilla-wafer crumbs, and confectioners' sugar in a bowl. Stir in melted butter.

Light pumpkin Bavarian cream fills a Gingersnap-Pecan Crumb Crust. The edge is decorated with pecan halves and a fleur-de-lis pattern of Chantilly Cream piped with a medium open-star ornamenting tube (see page 21).

71

TARTS

A tart is an open-faced pie with a freestanding shell that is usually made from a sweet tart pastry called *pâte sucrée* (sweet short paste).

The nature of the ingredients and the way they are combined produce a sweet crust that is tender, crumbly, and fragile rather than flaky. This rich pastry is quite suitable for delicate tart shells but is not sturdy enough to form a double-crust pie (flaky pastries are better for that).

The high percentage of butter, large amount of sugar, and viscosity of the egg yolks in sweet tart pastry produce a dough that is soft, moist, and sticky. This dough must be refrigerated at least 2 hours or until firm before rolling out. The dough can be made by hand or by machine (directions for both methods are given below).

SWEET TART PASTRY
Pâte sucrée

For a 9½- by 1-inch tart band or tin

1¼ cups flour
⅛ teaspoon salt
¼ cup sugar
2 extra-large egg yolks
½ teaspoon vanilla extract
6 tablespoons cold unsalted butter

For a 10-inch scalloped tart band or a 10- by 2-inch tart tin

1½ cups flour
¼ teaspoon salt
⅓ cup sugar
3 large egg yolks
½ teaspoon vanilla extract
½ cup cold unsalted butter

By Hand

1. Sift flour onto work surface; make a well in the center.

2. Place salt, sugar, egg yolks, and vanilla in center; mix with fork to dissolve sugar in yolks.

FROM TARTS TO TARTLETS

Tart tins come in a variety of shapes and sizes. Any tart less than 5 inches in diameter is usually called a tartlet. If it is boat-shaped, it's called a barquette. Most tart recipes (and all of the tart recipes in this book) are designed for a standard-sized tart tin (9½ by 1 inch). Such a tin holds between 2¾ and 3 cups of filling when it is lined with pastry.

Size of Tartlet Tin	Filling Needed	Approximate Number of Tartlets
9½" by 1" (round)	2¾ to 3 cups	1
4½" by ¾" (round)	⅓ to ½ cup	6
4½" by ½" (barquettes)	3 to 4 tbsp	14
2" by 1" (round)	1 to 2 tbsp	36 to 40

3. Pound butter with rolling pin to soften; add to yolks; mix butter with yolks, using fingertips or fork.

4. Using a dough scraper or pastry blender, gradually work flour into yolk mixture with a cutting motion to make coarse crumbs.

5. Gather crumbs into a rough mound. Work small portions of the dough against the work surface with the heel of your hand (pushing away from you). When pieces of dough are pliable and peel away from surface in one piece, press into a ball. Wrap well and refrigerate 2 hours or until firm.

In a Food Processor

Place salt, sugar, egg yolks, vanilla, and cold butter in bowl of food processor; process using 4 one-second pulses. Add flour and process with 6 to 8 one-second pulses, until dough begins to clump (but doesn't form a ball). Gather into a rough mound. Work small portions of the dough against the work surface with the heel of your hand (pushing away from you). When pieces of dough are pliable and peel away from surface in one piece, press into a ball. Wrap well and refrigerate 2 hours or until firm.

Rolling Out Tart Pastry

1. Remove dough from refrigerator; allow to soften slightly before rolling. Place dough on lightly floured surface; sprinkle a little flour on top of dough or rub some on rolling pin. Roll out dough from center toward edge to form a circle ⅛ inch thick and 1½ inches larger than your tart tin. Carefully lift dough and give a quarter turn after each rolling, reflouring surfaces as necessary to prevent sticking and tearing. Cupping hands slightly, occasionally reshape dough into a circle. If dough cracks or tears, brush a small, flat piece of dough with water and apply to tear as a patch. (It is better to patch dough than to reroll it because rerolling will toughen dough.)

2. To transfer dough to tart tin, place rolling pin just to one side of the center of the dough. Drape half of dough over the rolling pin; lightly rest dough across tart tin; unfold dough over tart tin. Lift edges of dough and carefully ease into tart tin. Gently mold dough to sides of tart tin with fingertips or a ball of dough. Trim dough even with top of tart band. Cover and refrigerate 1 hour. Tart shell may be frozen at this point.

NUT TART PASTRY

Nut pastry or *pâte sablée* is a sweet short pastry dough used to make pastry crust for tarts and tartlets or nut-sugar cookies. Once pâte sablée is baked, it has a sandy, crumbly texture and is very fragile. Vary the flavor by using different kinds of nuts in the recipe (almonds, hazelnuts, pecans, walnuts). Roll out scraps of leftover dough to form delicious nut-sugar cookies.

- ⅔ cup finely ground nuts
- ⅔ cup sifted confectioners' sugar
- ⅔ cup unsalted butter, softened
- 1 egg, lightly beaten
- ⅛ teaspoon salt
- 1⅔ cups flour (all-purpose or pastry)

By Hand

1. Combine ground nuts and confectioners' sugar in a medium bowl. Add soft butter and beat until light with electric beaters or wooden spoon.

2. Add egg and salt; beat until well mixed.

3. Add flour all at once and cut in with a pastry blender until just mixed. Press dough into a ball; flatten ball slightly with side of hand. Wrap well and refrigerate 4 hours or overnight.

In a Food Processor

1. Place ground nuts and confectioners' sugar in food processor fitted with steel blade and process until ground to a fine powder (not paste). Add soft butter and process until light and creamy.

2. Add egg and salt; process until well mixed.

3. Add flour all at once; process with 8 to 10 one-second pulses until just mixed (do not overmix).

4. Press dough into a ball; flatten slightly with side of hand. Wrap well and refrigerate 4 hours or overnight.

5. To roll out, see "Rolling Out Tart Pastry," page 72. Roll slightly thicker than ⅛ inch and handle gently. This dough is fragile and harder to work with than Sweet Tart Pastry.

FRESH FRUIT TART

A buttery, cookielike crust, vanilla pastry cream, and fresh fruit combine to create a classic fruit tart. Few pastries delight the eye and palate more than a tempting array of colorful fresh fruit tarts. The recipe below uses strawberries, kirsch-flavored pastry cream, and a red currant jelly glaze for a strawberry tart. When you vary the fruit, you'll want to select a flavoring and glaze that will complement or heighten the characteristic taste of the fruit. Consult the Flavor Pairings Chart (page 22) to choose an appropriate flavoring for the pastry cream. When glazing the tarts, choose a jam or jelly that matches your fruit in color and taste.

- 1 9½-inch Sweet Tart Pastry (see page 72)
- 1 cup milk
- 1 vanilla bean, split in half lengthwise, or 1 tsp vanilla extract
- 3 egg yolks
- ¼ cup sugar
- 3 tablespoons flour
- 1 tablespoon kirsch
- 3½ cups hulled, halved strawberries (1½ to 2 12-oz baskets)
- 1 cup red currant jelly
- 1 tablespoon kirsch

1. Roll out tart pastry and use it to line a 9½- by 1-inch tart tin with removable bottom. Blind-bake until fully baked (see page 60); cool.

2. To make pastry cream, bring milk to a boil in saucepan with vanilla bean; remove from heat and allow bean to steep in milk for 10 minutes. Remove vanilla bean, rinse it off, and let it dry (it can be reused one more time). If using vanilla extract, add in step 4.

3. Beat egg yolks and sugar together until thick and light. Stir in flour.

4. Reheat milk to boiling. Whisk milk into yolk mixture and return to the saucepan. Whisk over low heat until mixture boils; cook gently for 2 minutes, whisking constantly. Remove from heat and stir in vanilla extract (if using extract instead of vanilla bean). Transfer to a small container and cover surface of cream with a piece of buttered plastic wrap or parchment paper. Cool to room temperature and store in refrigerator until ready to use (will keep 2 to 3 days in refrigerator).

5. Stir 1 tablespoon kirsch into pastry cream. If pastry cream is too thick, fold in ½ cup stiffly whipped cream. Spread a ½-inch layer of pastry cream in bottom of fully baked tart shell.

6. Arrange a design of strawberries over the cream in concentric circles. You may use whole, halved, or sliced berries to form your design.

7. *To make glaze:* Heat jelly in a saucepan over low heat until just melted and bubbly. Stir in 1 tablespoon kirsch. Brush surface of strawberries with a thin layer of glaze. Reserve leftover glaze for another tart.

Serves 6 to 8.

When you're asked to bring dessert, surprise your friends with this striking and elegant Raspberry-Almond Tart.

RASPBERRY-ALMOND TART

This tart can be prepared hours before serving because the almond cream filling insulates the crust from the juicy berries. In addition, this tart lends itself to a myriad of fruit toppings: fresh strawberries, blueberries, sliced persimmons, sliced poached pears or peaches, kiwis, currants, fresh berries, mandarin orange segments, or poached rhubarb.

> 1 9½-inch Sweet Tart Pastry (see page 72)
> 7 tablespoons unsalted butter, softened
> 1¼ cups sifted confectioners' sugar
> 1¼ cups finely ground blanched almonds
> 1 small egg, lightly beaten
> 1 cup red currant or red raspberry jelly
> 1 tablespoon raspberry-flavored liqueur or kirsch
> 2 to 3 cups fresh raspberries (2 or 3 half-pint baskets)

1. Roll out tart pastry and use it to line a 9½-inch tart tin with removable bottom. Blind-bake until partially baked (see page 60); cool.

2. Preheat oven to 350° F. In a large bowl cream together butter and sugar. Stir in ground almonds. Add egg and stir until well mixed. Spread almond mixture evenly over bottom of partially baked tart shell. Bake for 25 to 30 minutes. Cool on wire rack.

3. Heat jelly in saucepan over low heat until just melted and bubbly. Stir in liqueur. Brush surface of tart filling with thin layer of warm jelly just before placing fruit on tart.

4. Arrange whole raspberries very close to one another in concentric circles on top of the filling. Reheat jelly and brush tops of berries lightly with jelly. Remove tart band and serve.

Serves 6 to 8.

LEMON CHESS TART

A delicate tart with subtle lemon flavor, this is a perfect dessert for summer. A lemon sablée crust adds texture and a taste of almonds.

*Lemon Sablée Pastry
(see page 57)*
1 tablespoon yellow cornmeal
¼ cup whipping cream
½ cup unsalted butter, room temperature
1 cup sugar
3 eggs
1 teaspoon finely grated lemon rind
1 teaspoon lemon juice
3 tablespoons confectioners' sugar
1½ cups Chantilly Cream (see page 59)

1. Roll out Lemon Sablée Pastry as for Sweet Tart Pastry (see page 72) and use it to line a 10-inch tart tin. Blind-bake tart shell until partially baked (see page 60). Tart shell should be set and just beginning to color. Remove from oven and allow to cool while you prepare filling.

2. Preheat oven to 350° F. In a small bowl stir cornmeal into cream; set aside.

3. In large bowl of electric mixer, cream butter and sugar until light and fluffy. Beat in eggs, one at a time, and continue beating until light. Stir in cornmeal mixture, lemon rind, and lemon juice.

4. Pour filling into shell almost to rim (do not overfill). Bake until custard is just set, about 30 minutes. When custard is set, center of tart will not move when tart is gently shaken from side to side, and a knife inserted in center will come out clean. (Cover edges of crust with foil, if necessary, to prevent overbrowning.)

5. Cool tart on wire rack. When cool, dust lightly with confectioner's sugar. Serve at room temperature with Chantilly Cream.

Serves 8.

APRICOT ALMOND TART

There should be a ditty: " 'Tis the season to bake apricots" sung throughout the land to herald the arrival and brief duration of apricot season in late June and early July. You'll enjoy fresh apricots most when they are baked unadorned on a buttery, crisp almond crust.

1 9½-inch Nut Tart Pastry (see page 73)
1 egg white, lightly beaten
4 cups halved, pitted apricots (2 lbs)
⅓ cup sugar
⅛ teaspoon ground nutmeg
2 tablespoons unsalted butter
¾ cup apricot preserves
1 tablespoon kirsch or orange-flavored liqueur
3 tablespoons toasted, sliced or slivered almonds (optional)

1. Preheat oven to 450° F. Roll out almond pastry and use it to line a 9½-inch tart tin with removable bottom. Brush inside of shell with egg white to moisture-proof.

2. Toss apricots with sugar and nutmeg. Arrange apricots cut side up (very close together and slightly overlapping) in pastry-lined tart tin. Dot with butter. Bake at 450° F for 15 minutes. Reduce heat to 350° F and bake until crust is golden brown and apricots are tender (30 to 40 minutes).

3. Heat preserves until melted; strain to remove pieces of fruit. Stir in liqueur. Brush tops of apricots liberally with warm preserves. Sprinkle with almonds, if desired. Remove tart band before serving.

Serves 6.

TO KEEP CRUST CRISP

A fruit tart that turns out to have a soggy crust is a bitter disappointment to the person who has worked so hard to make it. There are several ways to avoid the soggy crusts and diluted pastry creams that result from juicy fruits.

After baking the crust, use a pastry brush to paint the inside of the crust with a thin layer of melted currant jelly. This will in essence waterproof the crust.

If you have any vanilla cookies, ladyfingers, or stale white cake, you can crumble them up and sprinkle them over the pastry cream before topping it with the fruit. This will provide a dry barrier between the juicy fruit and the pastry cream and will help absorb the juices.

Be sure to dry fruit well with paper towels before placing on tart.

Assemble tart just before serving whenever possible.

APPLE CROSTADA

Apple crostada is the Italian version of old-fashioned apple pie. To produce this deep-dish tart, a 2-inch-deep tart tin is lined with a light, cookielike crostada crust, filled with thinly sliced apples, and topped with a layer of crust. It's delicious served warm but is also good served at room temperature. It will keep several days, and the crust tastes even better as it absorbs the apple juices.

        8 tablespoons unsalted butter,
           cut in 1-tablespoon pieces
        1 cup sugar
        2 eggs
        1 teaspoon vanilla extract
      1½ teaspoons baking powder
      2⅓ cups flour
        1 tablespoon butter
      2½ pounds tart apples (5 to 6
           apples; 8 cups sliced apples)
        ¼ cup lemon juice (juice of
           1 lemon)
        2 tablespoons sugar (optional)

1. *To make crostada dough in food processor:* Combine the 8 tablespoons butter, the 1 cup sugar, eggs, and vanilla in food processor fitted with steel blade. Process until well mixed and butter is reduced to ⅛-inch bits. Sift baking powder with flour; add to butter mixture in food processor. Process with 10 half-second pulses until dough is just mixed and can be gathered into a ball. Divide dough into two portions—one consisting of just over a third of the dough (for top crust), and the other just under two thirds of the dough (for bottom crust). Wrap each ball of dough in plastic wrap and refrigerate 1 hour. *To make dough by hand:* Follow the method for making Sweet Tart Pastry by hand, page 72.

2. Preheat oven to 400° F. Melt the 1 tablespoon butter and brush the inside of a 10- by 2-inch tart tin. You may substitute any 9- or 10-inch round pan, 2 to 3 inches deep, for the tart tin. A springform pan or regular 2-inch-deep cake pan will work well.

3. Peel, core, and thinly slice apples. Toss with lemon juice and the 2 tablespoons sugar, if desired. Omit sugar for a less sweet crostada.

4. On a well-floured surface roll out larger ball of crostada dough to a 12-inch circle, ¼ inch thick. Carefully fit dough into buttered tart tin. If dough tears, patch with scraps of dough. Fill with sliced apples. Roll out smaller piece of dough to an 11-inch circle, ¼ inch thick. Brush edges of bottom crust with water. Lay the 11-inch circle of dough on top. Trim edges to edge of tart tin. Press rim with the tines of a fork to score edges and seal them together.

5. Bake tart 20 minutes at 400° F. Reduce oven to 350° F and continue baking until crust is evenly browned, about 40 minutes longer. Allow to cool 30 minutes before serving. Serve warm with vanilla ice cream. Tart can be reheated for 10 to 15 minutes at 350° F, if you want to serve it warm after it has cooled completely.

Serves 8.

ORANGE CUSTARD TART

This is a tart for orange marmalade fans. The thinly sliced candied orange decorating the top is reminiscent of the bitter orange flavor found in orange marmalade. (See photo, page 52.)

        2 to 3 small seedless oranges
        1 cup water
        ¾ cup sugar
        1 9½-inch Sweet Tart Pastry
           (see page 72)
        3 eggs
        ⅔ cup sugar (scant)
        ¼ cup fresh orange juice
        1 teaspoon finely grated
           orange rind
        6 tablespoons unsalted butter,
           melted and cooled
        ½ cup apricot preserves
        1 tablespoon orange-flavored
           liqueur

1. Thinly slice oranges (¹⁄₁₆- to ⅛-inch slices) with very sharp knife.

In a wide saucepan combine water and the ¾ cup sugar; bring to a boil to dissolve sugar. Add orange slices and simmer over very low heat until translucent (about 45 minutes). Remove from heat and allow to stand in syrup overnight.

2. Roll out tart pastry and use it to line a 9½-inch tart tin with removable bottom. Blind-bake until partially baked (see page 60).

3. Preheat oven to 350° F. Combine eggs, the ⅔ cup sugar, orange juice, and orange rind in a mixing bowl; whisk until well mixed. Whisk in melted butter. Pour into partially baked tart shell and bake until custard is set (20 to 25 minutes). Cool to room temperature.

4. Decorate tart just before serving, if possible. Remove orange slices from syrup; drain well. Cut half of the slices in half. Cut the remaining slices in quarters. Arrange a row of overlapping quartered orange slices at the outer edge of the tart on top of the custard, with the rounded sides of the orange slices facing the edge of the tart. Then place a row of overlapping halved orange slices so they just overlap the tips of the first row. Continue with this pattern, alternating rows of quarters and halves, to the center of the tart. Form a very thin half-orange slice into a cone shape for the center decoration. The tart top should now resemble an opening petaled flower.

5. Heat preserves until melted; strain to remove solid pieces of fruit. Mix in liqueur. Brush glaze lightly over orange slices. Reserve any leftover glaze for another tart.

6. Remove tart tin and serve at room temperature. This tart should be stored in the refrigerator if not consumed within a few hours.

Serves 6 to 8.

LEMON TARTS

A versatile lemon curd that uses no starch for thickening can be used to fill tarts of many sizes. Soft butter, added at the last minute, thickens the curd. If the curd is poured immediately into prebaked tart or tartlet shells, it will cool with a shiny surface and easy-to-cut texture.

Decorate the tarts just before serving with slices of peeled fresh kiwi, peeled white grapes, or Cooked Meringue. This recipe will fill one 9½- by 1-inch tart shell, six 4½- by ¾-inch round tart shells, fourteen 4½- by ½-inch narrow boat-shaped shells, or thirty-six 2- by 1-inch round, bite-sized shells.

> 1 9½-inch Sweet Tart Pastry (see page 72; use double recipe if making any of the tartlets)
> 3 whole eggs
> 3 egg yolks
> 1 cup sugar
> ⅔ cup lemon juice
> 1 teaspoon finely grated lemon rind
> ½ cup unsalted butter, softened Peeled, sliced kiwi fruit or peeled white grapes (optional)

Cooked Meringue (optional)

> 3 egg whites
> 1 cup superfine sugar

1. Roll out tart pastry and line tart shell(s). Blind-bake shell(s) until fully baked (see page 60). Cool.

2. In a stainless steel bowl, combine eggs, yolks, sugar, lemon juice, and lemon rind. Place bowl over a pot of boiling water and whisk or stir over medium heat until the mixture thickens to the consistency of mayonnaise (5 minutes). Do not boil this mixture or eggs will curdle!

3. Remove from heat and quickly whisk in soft butter, 2 tablespoons at a time, until all butter is incorporated. Pour immediately into fully baked tart shell or tartlet shells. Allow to cool to room temperature before decorating.

Serves 6 to 8.

Cooked Meringue Place egg whites in a stainless steel bowl. Whisk in sugar all at once and immediately begin whisking egg whites over boiling water (double boiler style). Whisk until egg whites begin to hold a ribbon (about 8 minutes; see Glossary, page 123). Remove from heat and beat meringue with an electric mixer until it holds stiff peaks. Place meringue in pastry bag fitted with an open-star tip, and use to decorate Lemon Tarts.

Meringue and White Grape Tartlets Pipe Cooked Meringue on top of 4½-inch tartlets in the shape of an open-petaled daisy. Place a peeled white grape half inside each petal of the flower. Place meringue-topped tarts under the broiler for a few minutes until the meringue is light brown. Watch carefully to avoid scorching the meringue or exposed lemon filling.

These boat-shaped lemon tartlets are perfect for afternoon tea or coffee. The Cooked Meringue piped on top in an open-star pattern adds flair to this refreshing dessert.

77

This custard-filled pear tart is baked in a scallop-edged tart band. The top is dusted with confectioners' sugar to create a delicate flower pattern.

BAKED PEAR TART

This tart looks especially pretty when baked in a scalloped tart band. Thinly sliced pear halves radiate from the center to form the petals of a flower. After baking, the finishing touches reveal an orange-petaled daisy outlined by a delicate layer of sifted confectioners' sugar.

- 1 10-inch Sweet Tart Pastry for scalloped tart tin (see page 72)
- 6 tablespoons unsalted butter
- 1½ large eggs (beat second egg and use half)
- ½ cup plus 1 tablespoon granulated sugar
- 3 tablespoons sifted flour
- 4 ripe pears (Anjou or Bartlett)
- 2 tablespoons lemon juice
- ½ cup apricot preserves
- 1 tablespoon pear liqueur or water
- ¼ cup confectioners' sugar

1. Position a 10-inch scalloped tart band on a flat baking sheet. (You may substitute a 10-inch tart tin with removable bottom or 10-inch circular tart band.) Roll out tart pastry and line tart band or tin (see page 72). Trim dough even with the top of the tart band. Wrap and refrigerate 1 hour. Tart shell may be frozen at this point.

2. To make custard filling, melt butter over medium heat until the milk solids in it turn brown. Immediately remove from heat and allow to cool for 5 minutes. Place eggs in a mixing bowl and gradually whisk in granulated sugar. Whisk in flour. Whisk in melted butter and all of the brown bits that cling to the bottom of the pan (these give the tart a delicious nutty flavor and aroma). Set aside until tart is assembled.

3. Preheat the oven to 375° F. Peel the pears. Cut each in half lengthwise, remove core and seeds, and place into a large bowl of cold water with 2 tablespoons lemon juice (this keeps the pears white). Remove pear halves from water; dry well on paper towels. Using a sharp, thin knife held at a 45-degree angle to the board, slice each pear half crosswise in ⅛-inch slices, beginning at the narrow tip. Slide a narrow spatula under each sliced pear half, and transfer it to the pastry-lined tart band. Center each pear half in a "petal" of the tart band, with the narrow end of the pear pointing toward the center. Then push the pear slices from the narrow to the wide end of each pear to fan the slices slightly. Trim the tip off the last pear half, slice, and place in the center of the tart. Pour the custard filling in the empty spaces around, but not on top of, the pears. The custard should come only halfway up the side of the tart.

4. Bake for 20 minutes at 375° F. Reduce oven to 350° F and bake until custard looks fully cooked (40 to 50 minutes longer). If edges of crust begin to brown too much, cover them with strips of foil. Remove from oven and cool completely.

5. *To make the glaze:* Heat preserves over low heat until completely melted. Strain to remove pieces of fruit; stir in pear liqueur. When tart is cool, brush the pear halves with a thin coat. Then cover each pear half with an upside-down barquette tin (boat-shaped) with fluted sides. Cover the center pear with an upside-down small, round brioche tin or tartlet tin. Sift a light layer of confectioners' sugar over the tart. Carefully lift off the tins and you have a flower design on your tart . . . a flower within a flower!

6. Lift off the tart band, slide tart onto serving plate, and serve at room temperature.

Serves 8 to 10.

TOASTED NUT TART

This variation on pecan pie is easy to transport and will keep for a long time. Make one to take to the mountains on a ski trip.

- 1 9½-inch Sweet Tart Pastry (see page 72)
- ⅔ cup blanched almonds (whole or halved)
- ⅔ cup pecan halves
- ½ cup whole hazelnuts
- 2 large eggs, lightly beaten
- ⅓ cup dark brown sugar
- ⅔ cup light corn syrup
- ⅛ teaspoon salt
- 1 teaspoon vanilla extract
- 2 teaspoons sifted flour
- 2 tablespoons unsalted butter, melted and cooled

1. Roll out pastry and use it to line a 9½-inch tart tin with removable bottom. Blind-bake until partially baked (see page 60).

2. Preheat oven to 350° F. Slice whole almonds in half lengthwise. Place almonds and pecans on a baking sheet and toast nuts until very pale brown (7 minutes). Toast and skin hazelnuts (see page 67). Remove from oven and place in a metal colander with large holes. Rub nuts against colander to remove skins as much as possible. Slice hazelnuts in half lengthwise. (You may leave nuts whole, but the tart is easier to cut and eat if nuts are halved.)

3. Preheat oven to 375° F. In a medium bowl combine eggs, sugar, corn syrup, salt, and vanilla, and stir until well blended. Stir in flour. Stir in melted butter; then stir in nuts.

4. Pour filling into partially baked tart shell to within ⅛ inch of top. Bake until custard is just set (30 minutes). Cool on wire rack. Remove tart band before serving.

Serves 6 to 8.

PINE NUT CROSTADA

In Italy a tart is called a crostada. It takes its name from the pastry dough used to form its crust. Crostada pastry is similar to Sweet Tart Pastry, but is often lightened with baking powder. Here the crostada is also perfumed with orange and lemon rind and holds a typical Italian filling of almond cream and pine nuts.

- 2 tablespoons orange-flavored liqueur
- 2 tablespoons golden seedless raisins
- ⅓ cup milk
- 1 egg yolk
- 2 tablespoons granulated sugar
- 1 scant tablespoon sifted flour
- ¼ teaspoon vanilla extract
- 6 tablespoons unsalted butter, softened
- ¾ cup plus 2 tablespoons finely ground blanched almonds
- ¾ cup plus 2 tablespoons sifted confectioners' sugar
- 2 medium eggs
- 2 scant tablespoons sifted flour
- 1 tablespoon dark rum
- ½ cup pine nuts
- ½ cup apricot preserves
- 1 tablespoon orange-flavored liqueur

Crostada Pastry

- 1¾ cups flour
- 1 teaspoon baking powder
- ¼ teaspoon salt
- ½ cup sugar
- ½ teaspoon finely grated lemon rind
- ½ teaspoon finely grated orange rind
- 1 egg
- ⅔ cup cold butter

1. Prepare Crostada Pastry, roll out, and use it to line a 9½-inch tart tin with removable bottom.

2. Heat orange liqueur; pour over the raisins; set aside. Allow raisins to soak in liqueur while you prebake the tart shell and assemble the filling.

3. Blind-bake the crostada shell until partially baked (see page 60).

4. Bring milk to a simmer in a very small saucepan. Place the egg yolk and sugar in a small bowl and whisk until light. Whisk in the 1 tablespoon flour. Add the milk all at once and whisk to blend. Return mixture to saucepan and bring to a boil over medium heat, stirring constantly; boil for 30 seconds; whisk until smooth. Remove from heat, stir in vanilla, and pour into a small bowl. Cover the surface of the vanilla cream with buttered plastic wrap and set aside.

5. Preheat oven to 350° F. Place butter in a mixing bowl and beat until creamy. Add ground almonds and confectioners' sugar; beat until well mixed. Add eggs, one at a time, beating after each addition. Add the 2 tablespoons flour; stir until just mixed. Drain raisins, reserving orange liqueur. Add raisins and rum to the almond cream. Add the vanilla cream to this mixture.

6. Pour filling into the partially baked crostada shell (it should be three-quarters full). Sprinkle pine nuts over the entire surface of the filling. Bake until set and slightly puffed (20 to 25 minutes). Cover edges of tart with strips of foil, if necessary, to prevent overbrowning of crust. Cool on wire rack.

7. Heat preserves until melted; strain to remove solid pieces of fruit. Mix in 1 tablespoon reserved orange liqueur. Brush glaze lightly over pine nuts. Reserve any leftover glaze for another tart.

8. Remove tart tin and serve at room temperature.

Serves 6 to 8.

Crostada Pastry

By Hand

1. Sift flour and baking powder onto work surface; form a well in the center. Combine salt, sugar, lemon rind, orange rind, and egg in the well; stir to mix.

2. Pound butter with a rolling pin to soften; work butter into egg mixture (with fingertips or fork) until partially mixed. Then cut the wet ingredients into the flour with a pastry scraper or cutter.

3. Gather the dough into a rough ball. The dough will not really stick together at this point and it will look dry. To create a smooth dough, quickly push pieces of the dough against the work surface with the heel of your hand. When the dough is smooth and pliable, press into a ball, wrap well, and refrigerate 1 hour or until firm.

4. Roll out the dough on a lightly floured surface to form a circle that is ⅛ inch thick and 1½ inches larger in diameter than your tart tin (see page 72). Wrap well and refrigerate 1 hour. Tart shell may be frozen at this point.

In a Food Processor

Combine salt, sugar, lemon rind, orange rind, egg, and softened butter in bowl of food processor fitted with metal blade; process with 4 one-second pulses. Sift flour and baking powder together and add all at once; process with 8 to 10 one-second pulses. Remove dough from processor, gather into a rough ball, and continue with step 3 above.

(Clockwise from left to right):
Toasted Nut Tart (page 79),
Pine Nut Crostada (page
80), Perigordine Walnut
Tart (page 82).

PERIGORDINE WALNUT TART

This simple French walnut custard tart is designed to showcase the delicious fresh walnuts of an area of France called Perigord Noir. A pastry chef from this area was kind enough to share his special recipe.

*1 9½-inch Nut Tart
    Pastry (made with almonds)
    (see page 73)*
1 cup walnut pieces
1 cup sifted confectioners' sugar
*1 cup plus 1 tablespoon
    whipping cream*
1 egg, lightly beaten
*1 tablespoon vanilla extract
    or walnut liqueur*
1 egg white, lightly beaten
1 ounce semisweet chocolate
10 walnut halves
*1 tablespoon finely
    chopped walnuts*
*1½ cups Chantilly Cream
    (see page 59)*

1. Roll out tart pastry and use it to line a 9½-inch tart tin with removable bottom. Blind-bake until partially baked (see page 60); cool.

2. Preheat oven to 350° F. Grind ⅓ cup of the walnut pieces with ¼ cup of the confectioners' sugar to a fine powder. You may do this with a food processor fitted with steel blade or in the small jar of an electric blender. Place resulting powder in a sifter; repeat until all walnut pieces are ground. Sift powder. With remaining sugar, regrind any nut pieces that are too large to pass through sifter.

3. In a medium bowl combine ground nuts and confectioners' sugar with cream, lightly beaten egg, and vanilla; stir to blend.

4. Brush inside of tart shell with egg white to moisture-proof shell. Pour filling into tart. Bake until custard is set (30 minutes). Cool completely on wire rack.

5. Melt chocolate in small mixing bowl over a pan of hot water (or use a double boiler). Cool chocolate to 86° F; use instant-read thermometer to test. Make a paper piping cone from parchment paper or waxed paper. Fill with chocolate and cut a 1/16-inch tip (or use a small pastry bag fitted with a 1/16-inch writing tip). Fill the bag with the melted chocolate and place a dot of chocolate on the bottom of each walnut half and position walnuts equally spaced around edge of tart. There should be one walnut half for each serving. Then drizzle the remaining chocolate in an attractive pattern over the tart. (A repeating overlapping daisy pattern is one possibility.) Sprinkle entire tart with 1 tablespoon finely chopped nuts. Remove tart band. Serve small slices at room temperature with Chantilly Cream (tart is very rich).

Serves 8 to 10.

RHUBARB TART

Here is a tart that makes rhubarb look as good as it tastes. Rhubarb pieces, cooked until just tender but still shapely, are arranged in concentric rows to resemble the petals of an opening flower.

*1 9½-inch Sweet Tart
    Pastry (see page 72)*
*7 tablespoons unsalted
    butter, softened*
*1¼ cups sifted
    confectioners' sugar*
*1¼ cups finely ground
    blanched almonds*
1 small egg, lightly beaten
1 cup red currant jelly
1 tablespoon kirsch

Poached Rhubarb Pieces

10 stalks young rhubarb
2½ cups sugar
3¼ cups water

1. Roll out tart pastry and use it to line a 9½-inch tart tin with removable bottom. Blind-bake until partially baked (see page 60).

2. Preheat oven to 350° F. In a bowl cream together butter and sugar. Stir in ground almonds. Add egg and stir until well mixed. Spread almond mixture evenly over bottom of partially baked tart shell. Bake for 25 to 30 minutes. Cool on wire rack.

3. Prepare Poached Rhubarb Pieces. While they cool, heat jelly in saucepan over low heat until just melted and bubbly. Stir in kirsch. Brush surface of tart filling with thin layer of warm jelly just before placing fruit on tart.

4. Arrange first row of rhubarb at outer edge of tart, each piece slightly overlapping the previous one. Arrange next row the same way, overlapping the first row by ¼ inch. Continue placing fruit in overlapping concentric circles to the center of the tart. Heat remaining red currant jelly and brush surface of rhubarb with a thin layer of warm jelly. Serve at room temperature.

Serves 6 to 8.

Poached Rhubarb Pieces Wash rhubarb, trim ends, slice into 1¼- to 1½-inch pieces. Place sugar and water in a wide, nonreactive pan (about 9 by 3 inches); bring to a boil to dissolve sugar. Reduce heat; add half of the rhubarb pieces and simmer gently for 4 to 5 minutes (or until rhubarb is just tender but still holds its shape). Transfer to a flat dish and cool in a single layer. Poach the remaining rhubarb; cool. Remember that the rhubarb will continue to cook after it is removed from the sugar syrup, so don't overcook it during the poaching stage.

CHERRY CUSTARD TART
Cherry clafouti

Nut pastry, sweet red cherries, and custard are baked together to create a French *clafouti*. When fresh cherries are not available, you can substitute fresh sliced kiwis, poached pears or peaches, or fresh berries. Boysenberries, loganberries, or olallieberries make delicious clafoutis. Almonds are a good choice for the crust.

 1 9½-inch Nut Tart Pastry
    (see page 73)
 ½ *cup milk*
 ½ *cup whipping cream*
 2 *whole eggs*
 2 *egg yolks*
 ½ *cup sugar*
    Pinch ground nutmeg
 1 *tablespoon kirsch*
 1 *egg white, lightly beaten*
2¼ *cups pitted sweet red cherries*
 ¼ *cup confectioners' sugar*

1. Roll out tart pastry and use it to line a 9½-inch tart tin with removable bottom. Blind-bake until partially baked (see page 60); cool.

2. Preheat oven to 400° F. Bring milk to a simmer; add cream. In a mixing bowl whisk eggs, egg yolks, sugar, and nutmeg together. Add milk slowly; stir well to blend; cool. Stir in kirsch.

3. Brush tart shell with a thin layer of lightly beaten egg white. Arrange cherries (whole or cut in half) in an even layer over bottom of tart shell. Pour custard over cherries (do not fill more than three-fourths full).

4. Bake for 10 minutes at 400° F. Reduce heat to 325° F and bake until custard is set (about 35 minutes).

5. Sift confectioners' sugar over tart. Place under broiler to caramelize sugar. Watch carefully—sugar burns easily. Serve slightly warm.

Serves 6 to 8.

HUBBARD SQUASH TART

Serve this tempting deep-dish tart in place of the traditional pumpkin pie at Thanksgiving or Christmas. Its tender, flaky, freestanding crust holds a rich, creamy squash purée laced with cognac. Canned pumpkin can be used, but you'll miss the delicate taste of the fresh squash.

 1 *deep-dish Egg Pastry (see*
    page 57)
 ¾ *cup whipping cream*
 ¾ *cup milk*
 1 *cup firmly packed*
    dark brown sugar
 ½ *teaspoon ground cinnamon*
 ⅛ *teaspoon ground cloves*
 ½ *teaspoon ground ginger*
 4 *extra-large eggs, lightly beaten*
 2 *tablespoons Cognac*
2¼ *cups well-drained fresh*
    Hubbard squash or
    pumpkin purée
 1 *cup Chantilly Cream (see*
    page 59)
 8 *to 10 pecan halves,*
    lightly toasted

1. Roll out pastry and use it to line a 10- by 2-inch tart tin with removable bottom. Blind-bake until partially baked (see page 60).

2. Preheat oven to 350° F. In a large bowl combine whipping cream, milk, sugar, cinnamon, cloves, and ginger. Add eggs, Cognac, and Hubbard squash purée; stir. Taste and add more spices to suit your taste.

3. Pour custard into tart shell. Bake until custard is set (1 hour). Cool before decorating or cutting.

4. Place Chantilly Cream in pastry bag fitted with an open star tip. Pipe cream in decorative swirls at edge of tart. Place a toasted pecan half between or on each swirl.

Serves 10.

TO MAKE FRESH HUBBARD SQUASH OR PUMPKIN PURÉE

Technique 1 *Cut squash or pumpkin in half. Scrape out the seeds and strings. Place cut side down in a glass baking pan; add ⅛ inch water to pan. Bake at 350° F until the pulp inside the squash is tender (1½ hours). Remove from oven and scrape the pulp of the squash away from the skin. Purée this in a food mill or food processor. Place the purée in a fine-meshed sieve and drain well. You may freeze the purée after draining or use immediately. It takes about 3½ to 4 cups of undrained purée to produce the 2¼ cups drained purée required for the Hubbard Squash Tart.*

Technique 2 *Peel squash or pumpkin with a sharp knife. Cut into 2-inch chunks. Place the peeled squash in a vegetable steamer and steam until tender (20 to 30 minutes). When pieces are tender, purée as above. Drain well.*

   If you freeze the purée, thaw it in a fine-meshed sieve. A lot more water will drain off during the thawing process.

A red-hot metal skewer burns caramelized lines into the sugar on top of Mille-Feuilles. It features three layers of puff pastry filled with vanilla pastry cream.

Puff Pastry

Puff pastry (also called *pâte feuilletée*) holds the distinction of being the most versatile, intriguing, and delicious of all the pastry doughs. The method for making puff pastry converts basic ingredients (flour, salt, water, and butter) into a multilayered dough that can rise to up to ten times its original height when baked. Close inspection of the airy, golden brown pastry reveals hundreds of separate, crispy layers, one upon the other. A buttery taste and aroma complete the picture.

THE ATTRIBUTES OF PUFF PASTRY

Volumes could be written on the attributes of puff pastry and its many applications for sweet or savory pastries. It can be made into pastry cases for all sorts of fillings in many shapes and sizes, freestanding pastry decorations, pastry decorations for the outside of a pastry, hors d'oeuvres, cookies, and wrappers for meat, fish, cheese, and fruit *en croute*. You would think that a dough that serves so many purposes and merits such high acclaim would be part of every cook's repertoire. It easily can be, but many novice bakers shy away from puff pastry because at first glance it appears to be a temperamental dough requiring many time-consuming steps. This is true only if you make puff pastry with the wrong ingredients under adverse circumstances.

Admittedly, there are several steps involved in making puff pastry, but they are neither difficult nor time-consuming. Each step actually takes only 5 to 10 minutes to accomplish, but the dough rests in the refrigerator for about one hour between each step. If you subtract the resting time from the total amount of time needed to make the dough, you will see that you devote only 30 to 40 minutes of your time to actually making puff pastry.

Puff pastry dough is made from two basic elements: (1) a smooth, elastic dough called the *détrempe* and (2) a block of butter beaten until pliable. When the dough and the block of butter are the same temperature and consistency, the butter is wrapped up in the dough, and this lump of dough-wrapped butter is given six *turns*. To give the dough a turn, you simply roll it out into a rectangle, fold the rectangle in thirds like a business letter, and turn it a quarter turn (90 degrees) on the work surface. Each turn is an exact repetition of this rolling, folding, and turning process.

The end product of all this turning is "virgin puff pastry." This is puff pastry that has been given six turns and has not been rolled out, cut out, or shaped in any way. Some pastries require virgin puff pastry and some pastries can be made with puff pastry trimmings or scraps.

TIPS FOR SUCCESS WITH PUFF PASTRY

For best results in making puff pastry, remember to:

□ Make puff pastry during the coolest part of the day on a day when you plan to be home for several hours.

□ Chill work surface and rolling pin for 30 minutes. Chill the work surface by placing on it several blocks of Blue Ice or a rimmed baking sheet filled with ice cubes. Chill rolling pin in freezer.

□ Use ingredients recommended in recipe. A combination of pastry flour and all-purpose flour yields a dough that will roll out easily but that has enough gluten to be rolled out without tearing and baked without breaking. The resulting dough has enough strength to hold its shape when baked, but remains tender. You can use 50 percent pastry flour (soft flour) and 50 percent all-purpose flour (a combination of soft and hard flours) or 75 percent pastry flour and 25 percent hard flour (bread flour high in gluten). Fresh, cold, unsalted butter and ice water are essential.

□ Wrap butter in détrempe when they are both the same temperature and consistency.

□ Chill the dough between every two turns to firm up the butter and relax the gluten in the dough, making it easier to roll out without compressing the layers. The dough should also be allowed to rest in the refrigerator again just before it is baked so the baked puff pastry will maintain its original shape and size.

□ Bake at 450° F unless otherwise indicated. Always begin baking in a hot oven.

Rolling Dough, Cutting Dough, and Baking Dough

Rolling Lightly flour dry work surface and chilled rolling pin. Roll dough out when cool and firm. Do not press down hard on dough; roll it evenly. Always rest dough in refrigerator when indicated between turns.

Cutting Cut dough when cold with a sharp knife. Cut straight down into dough with a clean, sharp movement. Do not drag knife through warm dough or you will seal the layers of dough together at the edge, making it difficult for the dough to rise.

Baking Bake in heavy pans lined with parchment paper. Do not use black metal pans. Always begin baking in a hot oven.

Bake at a high temperature (425° F to 450° F) for maximum rise. Watch the progress of your pastry carefully as it bakes. After the pastry has risen to its maximum height and is set, lower the temperature to finish baking. Sometimes it is necessary to finish baking large, filled puff pastry cakes at 350° F (for a longer time) to ensure that all of the layers are fully done.

If you like, you can bake puff pastry in advance. To serve it warm, which is best, reheat at 350° F for 5 minutes to recrisp.

Cutting Baked Puff Pastries To make rectangular puff pastry cases, after baking the puff pastry, slice puff pastry horizontally with a serrated knife to create a pastry case with a top and bottom, like a box, that can be filled with a filling.

To serve pastry, cut with a serrated knife held at a 45-degree angle to the pastry. Use a gentle sawing motion. Take care when cutting because puff pastry is very fragile and flaky. Using a nonserrated knife may crush the pastry and cause it to splinter. There's nothing worse than ruining a pastry you've spent hours preparing.

Refrigerating or Freezing Puff Pastry

Unbaked Dough After four turns, the dough may be wrapped in plastic wrap and refrigerated for two to three days, or it may be wrapped well and frozen for one month. Thaw, wrapped, in refrigerator (several hours or overnight). It is best not to freeze pastry in a self-defrosting freezer for more than a week.

Unbaked Pastries After the dough is cut and shaped, let it rest for up to one hour in the refrigerator. Then it should either be baked immediately or frozen as follows: Place pastry on a tray, freeze, remove from tray, wrap well, and freeze for up to one month. Frozen puff pastry tart shells may be blind-baked without thawing. Other puff pastries should be thawed in the refrigerator until the surface of the dough is slightly thawed. Brush with egg wash and bake the partially thawed puff pastries (if egg wash is applied to frozen pastry, it will freeze immediately).

Baked Puff Pastries Cool completely, freeze on a tray until firm, wrap well or place in freezer containers, and freeze for six to eight weeks. Loosen wrapping and thaw at room temperature. Crisp pastry in 350° F oven for 5 to 10 minutes.

Where Can I Buy Ready-Made Puff Pastry?

Commercially produced pastry made with unsalted butter may be substituted for the pastry in these recipes. It is usually sold with four turns. It is sold in specialty food stores in the freezer section. Thaw as for homemade puff pastry (see left). You can sometimes order fresh puff pastry from your local pastry shop. Ask the pastry chef to make a piece for you with four turns.

In large cities, there are wholesale commissaries that produce raw puff pastry and other doughs for restaurants and pastry shops. They sometimes sell to retail customers with a minimum order. You could buy 10 pounds and share it with friends or freeze whatever you can't use within a few days.

Uses for Puff Pastry Trimmings

There's no need to throw away the trimmings left over after virgin puff pastry is cut. Instead, gather the scraps into a ball, wrap, and refrigerate for at least one hour. (It can be stored up to two days in the refrigerator or can be frozen for up to one month.) The scraps can then be rolled out into a sheet and used. All pastries can be made with virgin puff pastry, but in some cases the scraps will suffice. The following pastries work quite well with trimmings.

- Dessert bases: as a lid for Tarte Tatin, as a base for Gateau Saint-Honoré, or as one of the layers in a dessert
- Mille-Feuilles (Napoleons), Apple Jalousie
- Pastry cases (to be blind-baked): barquettes (boat-shaped tart shells) to hold sweet or savory fillings, *croustades* to hold a variety of fillings for a first course or entrée, round or rectangular tart cases to hold fresh or poached fruits, Raspberry-Rhubarb Tartlets

QUESTIONS ABOUT PUFF PASTRY

What causes pastry to shrink during baking?

- Cutting or handling puff pastry when dough is warm.
- Failing to allow puff pastry to rest in refrigerator just before baking.

What causes puff pastry to rise unevenly?

- Rolling out dough unevenly, and failing to line up edges and square up dough after each turn.
- Dragging knife through pastry in certain areas.
- Allowing egg wash to drip down sides of dough in some places.
- Uneven heat distribution in oven.

What causes puff pastry to be flat or heavy?

- Applying too much pressure to dough when rolling or giving the dough an excessive number of turns.
- Rolling out dough when it is very warm.
- Sealing edges of pastry together by cutting with a dragging motion or allowing egg wash to drip down sides of dough.

What causes thin strips of dough to rise and fall over?

- Rolling out narrow strips of dough that are too thick; roll dough no thicker than 1/8 inch.

What can I do to prevent a soggy crust in a fruit tart?

- If you have any ladyfingers or slightly stale genoise, you can crumble them up and sprinkle the crumbs over the pastry cream before you place the fruit on top. This will provide a barrier between the juicy fruit and the pastry cream.

CLASSIC PUFF PASTRY
Pàte feuilletée

> 1 cup plus 1 tablespoon
>   unbleached all-purpose
>   flour
> 1 cup plus 1 tablespoon
>   unbleached white pastry
>   flour
> 1 teaspoon salt
> 3½ tablespoons cold unsalted
>   butter
> ½ cup plus 1 tablespoon
>   ice water
> 1 cup cold unsalted butter

1. Place flours, salt, and the 3½ tablespoons butter (cut into small pieces) in bowl of food processor fitted with metal blade. Process with one-second pulses until butter is cut into the flour and resembles coarse meal. This may also be done by hand in a medium bowl with a wire pastry blender or two knives. Empty flour mixture into a bowl and sprinkle a scant ½ cup of the cold water over it; toss with fingertips to moisten flour. Add more water, a few drops at a time, until mixture is just moist enough to be gathered into a ball; knead two or three times to form a soft, smooth ball of dough.

2. Cut an X into top of dough, ½ inch deep, with a knife; wrap well. Refrigerate until firm (2 to 3 hours). Can be refrigerated overnight.

To Wrap Butter in Détrempe and Give Dough Six Turns

1. Remove détrempe (dough) from refrigerator. Allow to warm up slightly (10 minutes).

2. Place butter between two pieces of waxed paper on work surface and beat with rolling pin to soften. Beat until butter is pliable and smooth but still cold. Pat butter into a 6-inch square.

3. When détrempe (dough) and butter are the same temperature and consistency (test by inserting a finger into each), roll out the détrempe into a rounded cross shape (see illustration below) 12 inches in diameter on an ice-cold, lightly floured surface (marble is best). Roll edges of dough thinner than center.

4. Place square of butter in the center of the dough and wrap the dough around it as shown below.

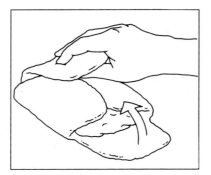

5. Return dough to refrigerator for 10 minutes if it has warmed up too much in wrapping process.

6. Place cool dough on a cold, lightly floured surface with vertical seam pointing toward you. Press dough down with rolling pin to flatten slightly. Begin rolling dough at end farthest from you, always rolling away from you, never sideways or toward you. Ease up on rolling pin when you come to ends of dough to avoid pushing butter out of the dough. As you roll out dough and fold it, keep sides and ends parallel and thickness even.

If butter breaks through the dough at any time during the rolling process, flour the problem areas generously and continue rolling dough.

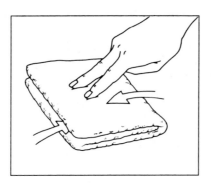

Turn 1 Roll dough into an 8- by 18-inch rectangle, with the short side facing you. Brush dough with soft pastry brush to remove flour. Fold the bottom third of the rectangle up (brush away any flour with pastry brush) and then fold the top third down, as if it were a business letter (see illustration below). Dust off excess flour and turn dough a quarter turn clockwise (90 degrees) so the seam is on your left. Square up the edges by tapping them with the rolling pin.

Turn 2 Roll out the dough as before. Fold in thirds as before (like a business letter). Square up edges of dough. Mark dough with two finger indentations to indicate number of turns. Wrap and refrigerate for 1 hour. After 1 hour proceed to turns 3 and 4. Do not store dough longer than 1 hour.

Turn 3 Remove dough from refrigerator and allow to warm slightly if very stiff and cold. Place seam on your left and roll and fold as for turns 1 and 2.

Turn 4 Turn dough a quarter turn clockwise (90 degrees) and roll and fold again. Mark dough with 4 finger indentations, wrap and refrigerate at least 1 hour or until ready to use. Dough can be frozen at this point or refrigerated 2 to 3 days.

Turns 5 and 6 Give dough 2 more turns and roll out to thickness specified in recipe. Cut or shape as directed. Rest 1 hour. Bake at 450° F unless otherwise indicated. After dough has been given 6 turns, it is best to roll it out, shape it, and either bake it or freeze the shaped dough. The best time to store the unshaped puff pastry dough is after 4 turns.

Makes 21 ounces puff pastry.

PUFF PASTRY TART BAND

Showcase fresh seasonal fruits in a puff pastry tart band. It's fun to create colorful combinations of flavors and textures by using more than one kind of fruit on your tart. Raspberries can be combined with blueberries, sliced figs, or fresh poached peaches, and kiwi slices look pretty with strawberries.

- 1¼ cups Pastry Cream (see page 102)
- ½ recipe Classic Puff Pastry (11 oz) with 6 turns (see page 88)
- 1 egg yolk lightly beaten with 1 teaspoon water (egg wash)
- 1 tablespoon fruit liqueur or brandy (see Flavor Pairings Chart, page 22)
- ¼ cup whipping cream or Crème Fraîche (see page 38)
- 3 cups fresh raspberries, hulled, halved strawberries, or sliced fruit
- ¼ cup apricot preserves, sieved (for light-colored fruits) or currant jelly (for dark fruits)
- 1 tablespoon liqueur or brandy

1. Prepare Pastry Cream and chill.

2. *To prepare tart band:* Roll out Classic Puff Pastry into a ⅛-inch-thick 8- by 16-inch rectangle. Cover and refrigerate until firm. Note: Puff pastry scraps may be used in place of virgin puff pastry to make tart band.

3. Cut out 3 cardboard templates with the following dimensions: 15½ inches by 5 inches, 15½ inches by ⅞ inch, and 3¼ inches by ⅞ inch.

4. When dough is well chilled, use cardboard templates and a long, sharp knife to cut out one 15½- by 5-inch rectangle of dough for tart base, two 15½- by ⅞-inch strips of dough for side walls of tart, and two 3¼- by ⅞-inch strips of dough for ends of tart.

5. Place large rectangle of puff pastry (base) on a parchment-lined baking sheet. Prick all over with fork.

Brush 1-inch border at edge of dough with cold water. Place thin strips of dough on moistened border to form tart walls and lightly press into place. Score edges of tart with back of small knife (making ⅛-inch-deep marks every ¼ inch along border). Cover and refrigerate 30 minutes.

6. Preheat oven to 425° F. Brush top only of narrow strips (walls) with egg wash. Bake 20 minutes or until tart is puffed and light brown. Lower oven to 400° F and bake until done (golden brown). Cool completely on wire rack before filling.

7. *To assemble tart:* Stir liqueur into Pastry Cream with a wooden spoon. Fold in stiffly whipped cream. Spread a ¼-inch layer of cream on bottom of tart. Arrange fresh fruit on top of cream. Melt preserves or jelly in small saucepan until bubbly; stir in liqueur or brandy to make glaze. Brush the glaze over the fruit.

Serves 6.

This fresh fruit tart band is filled with pastry cream, topped with peach halves and blueberries, and then glazed with apricot jam. This dessert can be made with almost any fruits in season.

RASPBERRY-RHUBARB TARTLETS

Raspberry-rhubarb compote, ginger cream, and Chantilly Cream are served in warm puff pastry shells. The warm pastry and cool fillings make a delightful combination. Puff pastry trimmings may be used in place of virgin puff pastry. Fresh strawberries (quartered) or diced fresh pineapple can replace raspberries in this recipe. You may also use all rhubarb for the compote. To do this, double the amount of rhubarb and sugar.

> 1 recipe Classic Puff Pastry (21 oz) with 6 turns (see page 88)
> 4 cups 1-inch rhubarb pieces (1 lb)
> ⅔ cup sugar
> ¼ teaspoon finely grated fresh ginger or ⅛ teaspoon ground ginger
> ½ teaspoon finely grated lemon rind
> 2 cups fresh raspberries (1½ to 2 half-pint baskets)
> 1½ cups Chantilly Cream (see page 59)

Ginger Pastry Cream

> 1 inch-long piece of fresh ginger
> 2 cups milk
> 6 egg yolks
> ½ cup sugar
> 3 tablespoons cornstarch, sifted
> 2 tablespoons unsalted butter, softened

1. Prepare Ginger Pastry Cream; chill well.

2. *To prepare tartlet shells:* Roll out Classic Puff Pastry to a thickness of ⅛ inch. Chill until sheet of dough is very firm (about 20 minutes). Cut out eight 5½-inch circles of dough; prick all over with a fork. Line 4½-inch tins with removable bottoms with circles of dough; refrigerate until firm.

3. When dough is firm, press against sides of tins to conform to the fluted sides; trim top edge, allowing dough to extend ⅛ inch above tin.

Wrap well and refrigerate 1 hour. Shells may be frozen at this point. See page 55 for freezing tips.

4. Preheat oven to 450° F. Blind-bake shells 15 to 20 minutes or until crust begins to set (see page 60 for blind-baking method). Reduce oven to 425° F, remove weights, and continue baking until golden brown. Remove from tins; fill as directed below. If you wish to bake tartlet shells in advance, reheat them on a baking sheet for 5 minutes at 350° F.

5. *To prepare compote:* Choose slender, young rhubarb stalks; wash well and cut into 1-inch pieces (to measure 4 cups). Combine rhubarb, sugar, ginger, and lemon rind in a non-aluminum saucepan; cover and cook over low heat until rhubarb is just tender.

6. Remove from heat; pour into a medium glass or ceramic bowl. Gently fold half of the raspberries into the rhubarb, taking care to keep raspberries whole. Cool to room temperature; fold in remaining raspberries. Refrigerate until ready to serve.

7. *To assemble tartlets:* Stir Ginger Pastry Cream until smooth. Spoon ¼ cup pastry cream into each warm tartlet shell. Cover with ½ cup raspberry-rhubarb compote. Top each with a dollop (2 to 3 tablespoons) of Chantilly Cream. Serve immediately while tartlets are still warm.

Makes 8 tartlets.

Ginger Pastry Cream

1. Peel ginger root; slice into 1/16-inch rounds. Combine ginger slices and milk in a saucepan; bring to a simmer. Remove from heat and allow ginger to steep in milk 10 minutes. Strain milk and discard ginger slices; return milk to saucepan.

2. In a medium bowl combine egg yolks and sugar; whisk until light and fluffy. Whisk in cornstarch. Bring milk back to a simmer; whisk milk into yolk mixture.

3. Return the mixture to the saucepan; bring to a boil over medium heat, stirring constantly. Boil 1 minute, whisking vigorously until cream is smooth. Remove from heat and whisk in butter. Pour into a clean bowl and place a piece of buttered plastic wrap directly on surface of cream. Cool to room temperature; refrigerate until ready to use. Will keep for 2 days in refrigerator.

BRIE OR CAMEMBERT IN PUFF PASTRY

Soft, ripened cheeses, such as a round of Brie or Camembert, are a special treat when baked in puff pastry. Wedges of the pastry served with a glass of wine and fresh fruit are perfect after dinner. You can enclose any size wheel of Brie or Camembert in puff pastry. Allow 2 ounces of cheese per person for a small serving. One recipe of puff pastry can easily enclose a 1-pound wheel of cheese.

You can make circles of puff pastry from 1½ pounds virgin puff pastry and use trimmings for decorating the outside of the pastry.

> 1½ recipes Classic Puff Pastry (2 lbs) with 6 turns (see page 88)
> 2 4-inch wheels (8 oz each) Brie or Camembert, well-chilled, or one 8-inch wheel (16 oz)
> 1 egg lightly beaten with 1 teaspoon water

1. Roll out Classic Puff Pastry 3/16 inch thick. Chill sheet of dough until firm. If using two 4-inch wheels of cheese, cut out two 6-inch circles and two 7-inch circles of puff pastry. If using one 8-inch wheel, cut out one 10-inch circle and one 11-inch circle. Cover and refrigerate 30 minutes. Gather scraps of dough into a ball; refrigerate 30 minutes.

2. Roll out trimmings of dough to ¹⁄₁₆ inch thick; freeze until very cold but not frozen. Use pastry cutters or sharp knife to make cutouts for decorating top of puff pastry (stems, leaves, flowers, grapes, etc.). Freeze decorations until firm. Freeze wheels of cheese for 20 minutes (no longer).

3. Place the two 6-inch circles (or one 10-inch circle) of puff pastry on a parchment-lined baking sheet. Place a wheel of cheese in center of each. Brush water around the border from the cheese to edge of pastry. Cover each wheel with a 7-inch circle of puff pastry dough (or the 11-inch circle if using the larger wheel of cheese). Press down on dough around base of cheese with fingertips to seal edges of dough together. Place in freezer 10 minutes to firm dough.

4. When dough is well chilled but not frozen, cut a scallop pattern at edge of pastry with a sharp knife. Create a hollow foil tube (a chimney) by wrapping a 1-inch by 1½-inch strip of foil 2 or 3 times around a pencil; butter exterior of foil tube and remove pencil. Cut a ¼-inch hole in center of top layer of pastry and fit the buttered aluminum foil tube into it. This will allow the steam from inside the pastry to escape. Brush cutout decorations with water and apply in an attractive pattern on top. Return to freezer for 20 minutes. Preheat oven to 425° F.

5. Remove pastry rounds from freezer, brush top of each with egg wash (take care not to drip any down the sides of the pastry). Bake until golden brown (20 to 25 minutes). Cool for 30 to 45 minutes before cutting. If served immediately, the cheese will run out after the pastry is cut. Cut each pastry into 4 wedges.

Serves 8.

Step·by·step

WORKING WITH PUFF PASTRY

Soft, ripened cheeses such as Brie or Camembert are a special treat when baked in puff pastry. Here we show you the steps involved in preparing Brie in Puff Pastry.

These cheeses are sold in wheels with a white, soft crust that is completely edible. Inspect the crust and choose a wheel of cheese that has a mild smell and a snowy white crust that is completely intact.

1. Center wheel of Brie on top of smaller circle of puff pastry. Brush water on pastry from cheese to edge of pastry. Place larger circle of pastry on top and press gently on top piece of dough at edges to seal the two circles together. Place in freezer until dough is firm but not frozen, about 10 minutes.

2. Use a small, sharp knife to cut a scallop pattern around edge of dough. Gather scraps of dough into a ball; chill until firm. Roll out scraps to ¹⁄₁₆-inch thickness; chill well. Use cookie cutters or sharp knife to cut out decorations for top of pastry.

3. Cut a ¼-inch hole in center of pastry (do not puncture cheese). Wrap a 1-inch by 1½-inch piece of foil around a pencil to form a tube of foil (chimney). Place this tube in hole in center of pastry to act as a steam vent. Brush pastry cutouts with water and apply to top. Place in freezer 20 minutes.

4. Remove from freezer. Brush top of pastry with egg wash. Bake 20 to 25 minutes at 425° F.

TARTE TATIN

Jean Bertranou, former owner of L'Ermitage restaurant in Los Angeles, created this version of the marvelous, caramelized, upside-down confection known as Tarte Tatin. This tart has been famous throughout France, and especially in Paris, for nearly a hundred years. It is distinguished from the traditional French tart by the way it is made—with the crust on top. The Tatin sisters, who developed the recipe, were too poor to have an oven, so they cooked the tart on top of the stove. The apples were placed on the bottom of the heavy-bottomed pan on the burner so that they would absorb more of the heat and thereby protect the more delicate crust on top, which cooks more quickly.

Particularly beautiful when un-molded, this version stands taller than most tartes Tatin, and the apples are a rich, rose-toned caramel. This tart is very good warm and may stand at room temperature for hours. You can reheat it successfully just before serving (10 minutes at 350° F). Serve with Crème Fraîche (see page 38) or whipped cream on the side.

- 1 10-inch circle of puff pastry, ⅛ inch thick (approximately 7 oz or ⅓ of Classic Puff Pastry recipe, page 88)
- 1 cup unsalted butter, softened
- 1½ cups sugar
- 12 to 16 Red Delicious apples, peeled, cored, and halved (about 9 lbs)
- 1 cup Crème Fraîche (see page 38) or Chantilly Cream (see page 59)

1. Prepare puff pastry circle and prick it all over. Refrigerate until needed. Line one burner well on top of your stove with aluminum foil to catch any juices that might spill over.

2. Use a deep, heavy-bottomed pan (preferably copper) with straight sides and an ovenproof handle. It must be at least 3½ inches deep and 9½ to 10 inches in diameter. Cover the bottom of the pan complete-ly with the butter. Sprinkle sugar evenly over butter. Stand apple halves (10 to 14 will fit) in pan, large end down, with the cut side of each half touching the back of the apple half in front of it, and the sides touching the edge of pan. Place 2 apple halves facing each other in center of pan. Completely fill space between outer and center cir-cles with apple halves. Pile as many apple halves as possible on top of these apples.

3. Place pan over medium-high heat, bring to a boil, and cook until apples become pliable and exude juices. After about 20 minutes, the juices will boil up the sides of the pan. At this point, remove from heat until bub-bling subsides (5 minutes). Use a fork and a long, narrow spatula to fit in some of the apples piled on top. Be sure to distribute the new apples evenly around the tart so they do not all end up in one place.

4. Return pan to stove and continue cooking, removing from the heat about every 20 minutes to insert more apples until all that will fit have been inserted. If juices boil over too much (usually occurs about 40 min-utes after starting), with a bulb baster remove 1 cup juices to a saucepan and reserve. Continue cooking until the juices around the apples begin to turn golden brown and caramelize (about 1½ hours after start). Now boil down any syrup you removed until it is the same caramel color as the juice around the apples and add it back to pan with apples. Cook until the syrup and apples are a deep, golden brown, taking care not to burn the sugar at this point. Remove from heat for 5 to 10 minutes.

5. Preheat oven to 450° F. Place the circle of pastry on top of the apple mixture. Bake in oven until pastry is done (about 30 minutes).

6. Remove Tarte Tatin from the oven and allow to stand for 10 min-utes. Place a round platter over top of pan and carefully invert, leaving pan intact.

Note The finished tart in the copper pan is very heavy and can be difficult to invert. Don't be surprised if you need help doing it. Hot caramel burns if you spill it on your skin. Tilt plate away from you when inverting tart; use an oven mitt on hand hold-ing pan and a rubber glove on hand under plate.

Allow to stand undisturbed for 10 more minutes, then remove pan. If some of the apples fall over, butter your hands and straighten them out to make a nice, even tart. Use a bulb baster to remove excess juices from plate under tart. If you want the tart to be shinier, glaze it with this excess juice or with apple jelly. In both cases, the glaze should be warmed and applied with a pastry brush or spatula. Applejack or Calvados can be added to this glaze before brushing on tart.

A classic French dessert, Tarte Tatin is a caramelized apple tart that is baked in a pan then turned upside down. This tart is especially delicious served warm.

APPLE JALOUSIE

This double-crusted rectangular puff pastry tart has an apple/apricot filling that peeks through little slits in the top layer of puff pastry. For variety, substitute ⅓ cup thick raspberry, strawberry, blackberry, blueberry, or cherry preserves for the apple filling.

- ½ recipe Classic Puff Pastry (11 oz) with 6 turns (see page 88)
- 3 Golden Delicious apples, peeled, cored, and thinly sliced
- 3 tablespoons unsalted butter
- 2 tablespoons sugar
- ¼ teaspoon vanilla extract
- ¼ teaspoon ground cinnamon
- 1 teaspoon lemon juice
- ¼ teaspoon finely grated lemon rind
- 3 tablespoons apricot preserves
- 1 tablespoon orange-flavored liqueur
- 1 egg beaten with 1 teaspoon water (egg wash)
- 1 egg white, beaten with 2 teaspoons water until frothy (optional)
- 2 tablespoons sugar (optional)

1. Roll out Classic Puff Pastry into a 10- by 14-inch rectangle, ⅛ inch thick. Cut rectangle in half lengthwise to create two 5- by 14-inch rectangles (trim edges to form perfectly straight sides). Place on baking sheet, cover, and chill while you prepare filling.

2. *To prepare filling:* Place apples in saucepan with butter. Sprinkle with sugar and add vanilla, cinnamon, lemon juice, and lemon rind. Cover with a circle of parchment paper and then with lid. Sweat apples over low heat until just tender (15 to 20 minutes). Stir in apricot preserves and orange liqueur. Remove from heat; cool completely.

3. *To assemble:* When filling is cool, remove puff pastry rectangles from refrigerator. Place one piece of dough on a parchment-lined baking sheet. Spoon filling down center, leaving a 1-inch border all around the edge. Brush border with egg wash (egg beaten with water).

4. Fold the other rectangle of dough in half lengthwise and, with a sharp knife, cut across the fold every ⅜ inch with the heel of the knife (the fat end) to within 1 inch of the outer edge.

5. Lift the cut rectangle and place with folded edge in the center on top of the other piece. Unfold over filling and press down on edges all around to seal to bottom layer of pastry. Trim edges, if necessary, to neaten them. Score edges of jalousie with the back of a small knife (making ⅛-inch-deep marks every ¼ inch along edges). Cover and chill 30 minutes in refrigerator.

6. Preheat oven to 425° F. If you want a shiny glaze, brush top of pastry with egg wash and bake in oven until puffed and golden brown (30 to 40 minutes). For a sugared top, remove pastry from oven 5 to 10 minutes before the end of baking, brush the top with egg white beaten with water, and sprinkle generously with sugar. Continue baking until done. Serve warm or at room temperature. Delicious with Chantilly Cream (see page 59) or vanilla ice cream.

Serves 6 to 8.

STRAWBERRY FEUILLANTINES

Feuillantines are rectangles of puff pastry that are decorated and baked to form pastry cases. These elegant containers hold kirsch-flavored pastry cream, fresh strawberries or raspberries, and Chantilly Cream. A perfect pastry to follow any dinner party.

- 1¼ cups Pastry Cream (see page 102)
- 1 recipe Classic Puff Pastry (21 oz) with 6 turns (see page 88)
- 1 egg yolk lightly beaten with 1 teaspoon water
- 1 tablespoon kirsch or other liqueur
- 4½ cups halved or quartered fresh strawberries or fresh raspberries
- 2½ cups Chantilly Cream (see page 59)

1. Prepare Pastry Cream and chill.

2. *To prepare feuillantines:* Roll out Classic Puff Pastry into a 12- by 14-inch rectangle that is ¼ inch thick. Place on a parchment-lined baking sheet and refrigerate until very firm (about 20 minutes).

3. Meanwhile cut out a cardboard rectangle that is 2¾ inches by 5 inches to use as a pattern. Using this pattern, cut out 8 rectangles of puff pastry from chilled dough with a sharp knife. Turn each rectangle of dough over and place on parchment-lined baking sheet. Cover and refrigerate 1 hour.

4. Gather scraps into a ball; chill. When scraps are firm, roll out to a thickness of ¹/₁₆ inch. Place on a baking sheet and freeze briefly to chill dough. Cut out small leaves, flowers, stems, and other designs from dough to decorate tops of rectangles. Brush the rectangles (top only) with egg wash. Arrange cutouts decoratively on top of each rectangle. Chill 20 minutes. Rectangles may be frozen at this point. To thaw, see page 55.

5. Preheat oven to 425° F. Brush top only of each rectangle with egg wash. Bake feuillantines 20 minutes. Lower oven to 400° F and continue baking until done (golden brown). Allow to cool on wire racks. Store in dry place at room temperature (or in a warming oven) until ready to fill.

6. *To assemble:* Split each rectangle in half horizontally with a serrated knife, creating a bottom and a top for each rectangle. Remove any uncooked dough from center. Place bottoms of rectangles on dessert plates.

7. Stir kirsch or other liqueur into the Pastry Cream. Spoon 2 tablespoons Pastry Cream into bottom of each rectangular pastry case. Sprinkle fresh berries on top of cream.

8. Prepare Chantilly Cream. (For a rich, sweet-tart taste, substitute Crème Fraîche for whipping cream in Chantilly Cream recipe—see page 59.) Place Chantilly Cream in a pastry bag fitted with a large, open-star tip. Pipe a layer of rosettes on top of berries. Place puff pastry tops on filled pastry cases. Decorate plate with a few berries. Serve immediately, while pastry is still warm.

Makes 8 pastries.

Here is a variation of the delicate Strawberry Feuillantines that uses raspberries instead of strawberries. A puff pastry rectangle is baked, then split horizontally and filled with vanilla pastry cream, raspberries, and Chantilly Cream or whipped Crème Fraîche. Use a medium open-star tip to pipe the cream.

95

MILLE-FEUILLES

Mille-Feuilles translates from the French into "a thousand leaves," and that is precisely what you get—thin, delicate leaves of puff pastry are layered with rum pastry cream to form the base for Mille-Feuilles and Napoleons. Both begin with a long, narrow pastry that is either dusted with confectioners' sugar (for Mille-Feuilles) or iced with marbled fondant (for Napoleons). This is assembled as a large pastry and then later cut into small servings. It is best when assembled just before serving. Puff pastry trimmings may be used for Mille-Feuilles in place of virgin puff pastry. People are less familiar with Mille-Feuilles than with Napoleons, but actually they are easier to prepare and equally delightful. (See photo, page 86.)

> 2½ cups Pastry Cream (see page 102)
> 1 recipe Classic Puff Pastry (21 oz) with 6 turns (see page 88)
> 1 cup apricot jam, melted and sieved
> 2 teaspoons rum
> ¼ cup whipping cream
> 1 cup toasted sliced almonds, coarsely chopped
> ⅓ cup confectioners' sugar

1. Prepare Pastry Cream and chill.

2. *To prepare puff pastry rectangle:* Roll out Classic Puff Pastry into a 12- by 18-inch rectangle, ⅛ inch thick; chill until firm (about 20 minutes). Cut into 3 equal rectangles that measure 6 inches by 12 inches each. Prick each rectangle all over. Place on parchment-lined baking sheets, cover and refrigerate 30 minutes. If you have an oven and baking sheets that will accommodate the 12- by 18-inch sheet of puff pastry, this sheet can be pricked all over and baked whole. Then, after baking, it can be cut into 3 equal strips with a serrated knife.

3. Preheat oven to 425° F. Cover pastry strips or whole sheet with parchment paper. Set another baking sheet on top of each pastry layer to weight dough. Bake for 10 minutes. Lift up top baking sheet(s) and parchment paper; prick the dough again; replace top baking sheets and parchment and bake 5 minutes more. Reprick dough. When pastry is browning and appears to be set, remove baking pans and parchment paper from top of pastry. When pastry is crisp, golden brown, and thoroughly baked, remove from oven. Cool on wire racks.

4. *To assemble:* Trim pastry rectangles with a serrated knife so they are all the same size. Reserve the flattest layer for the top. Cut out a cardboard rectangle slightly smaller than your puff pastry rectangles to use as a base for the cake. Wrap cardboard with foil.

5. Place one of the 3 pieces of puff pastry on the foil-wrapped cardboard. Brush this pastry with a thin layer of warm apricot jam. Stir the rum into the Pastry Cream. Stiffly whip cream and fold into Pastry Cream (see Note).

6. Spread half of the cream on the first layer of pastry. Place the second layer on top. Brush with a thin layer of jam. Spread all but ¼ cup of the remaining cream on second layer. Place the third layer of pastry on top with smoothest side up. Ice the long sides of the cake with the remaining cream and press the toasted almonds on the sides.

7. Sift a 1/16-inch layer of confectioners' sugar evenly over top of cake. Heat a long metal skewer over your stove burner (gas burners work best) until red-hot. Hold skewer at a 45-degree angle to the long sides of the cake with point angled toward the top left corner of the cake. Burn lines in the confectioners' sugar 1½ inches apart on top of cake. Reheat skewer as necessary to create dark caramelized lines in the sugar.

To create a cross-hatch pattern, burn another set of lines beginning with skewer angled towards the upper right corner of cake.

Serves 6.

<u>Note</u> If you must assemble the cake several hours before serving, you can add a small amount of gelatin to the Pastry Cream. Sprinkle 2 teaspoons gelatin over 2 tablespoons water or rum. When gelatin is spongy, place bowl over hot water (double boiler) and stir to dissolve gelatin. Cool over ice until syrupy. Stir into Pastry Cream just before folding in whipped cream.

Raspberry Mille-Feuilles Mille-Feuilles can also be filled with fresh raspberries and Chantilly Cream. Dissolve 2 teaspoons gelatin in rum or water as directed in the Note above. Using Chantilly Cream recipe on page 59, whisk dissolved gelatin into whipping cream along with sugar and vanilla when cream just begins to thicken. Fold 1½ cups fresh berries into 2½ cups of the cream. Use this filling to replace rum pastry cream in recipe above. Use red raspberry jelly or red currant jelly in place of apricot jam. To finish top, dust top layer of pastry with a thin layer of confectioners' sugar before layer is put on cake. Place under broiler to create a shiny, caramelized-sugar top; cool completely before setting on cake. Ice long sides with ½ cup Chantilly Cream; press toasted almonds onto sides. Pipe 6 Chantilly Cream rosettes down center of cake to mark each Mille-Feuilles. Place a raspberry in center of each rosette. Slice as above.

PITHIVIERS
Almond-filled puff pastry

This version of the classic almond-filled puff pastry cake turns out perfect every time. Remember to allow the puff pastry to chill in the refrigerator when indicated. Freezing the Almond Pastry Cream before filling the cake prevents the cream from leaking out of the cake during baking. This cake is as delicious for breakfast as it is for dessert.

1 recipe Classic Puff Pastry (21 oz) with 6 turns (see page 88)

1 egg beaten with 1 teaspoon water (egg wash)

1 tablespoon confectioners' sugar

Pastry Cream

2 small egg yolks or 1½ large egg yolks

2 tablespoons sugar

1 tablespoon cornstarch, sifted

½ cup milk

½ teaspoon vanilla extract

Almond Pastry Cream

2½ tablespoons unsalted butter, softened

¾ cup finely ground blanched almonds (almond meal)

¾ cup sifted confectioners' sugar

1 egg yolk

1 tablespoon dark rum

¼ teaspoon almond extract

¼ cup Pastry Cream

1. Prepare Pastry Cream, then use it to prepare Almond Pastry Cream.

2. Roll Classic Puff Pastry into a 9-by 18-inch rectangle. Cut into two 9-inch squares. Roll out one square slightly larger than the other. Place both squares on a baking sheet; cover and refrigerate until firm (about 20 minutes).

3. Place smaller square of dough on a parchment-lined baking sheet. With an inverted 8-inch-diameter round cake pan, lightly press a circular impression in the center of the square. Then place the Almond Pastry Cream in the center of this circle and spread evenly, leaving a 1-inch margin at the edge of the circle.

4. Brush the dough outside the almond cream with egg wash to edges of square. Place the larger square on top. Press down edges to seal. Refrigerate until dough is firm enough to cut easily (about 20 minutes).

5. Center an 8-inch-diameter round cake pan upside down over the dough. With a very sharp knife, cut a ¾-inch scalloped border design all the way through the pastry around the circumference of the circle to create a scalloped edge to the pastry. Cake may be frozen at this point.

6. Cut a ¼-inch hole in center of top layer of pastry and fit with a buttered aluminum foil chimney (see step 4 of Brie or Camembert in Puff Pastry, page 93). This will allow the steam from inside the pastry to escape. Cover and refrigerate 30 minutes.

7. Preheat oven to 450° F. Lightly brush top of cake with egg wash. Do not allow any egg wash to drip down the sides. With the back of the tip of a small, sharp knife, lightly score top of cake with spiraling semicircles (about ½ inch apart). Begin at chimney in center and curve your lines out to the edge.

8. Bake until the pastry has risen and is light brown (20 minutes). Then reduce oven to 400° F and bake until done (about 40 minutes). If the cake is browning too quickly, cover top with a sheet of parchment paper or aluminum foil. It is sometimes necessary to reduce temperature to 350° F and continue baking in order to bake inner layers completely.

9. After baking, remove foil chimney and sift confectioner's sugar over top. Place under broiler or in very hot oven for a few minutes until confectioners' sugar melts and caramelizes into a shiny glaze. Watch constantly to avoid burning top.

10. Serve within a few hours after baking. If you must hold the pastry longer, reheat in a 350° F oven for 5 to 10 minutes.

Serves 6.

Pastry Cream

1. Place the egg yolks in a small bowl. Gradually add sugar and beat until thick and pale yellow. Whisk in cornstarch.

2. Bring milk to a simmer and whisk into egg yolk mixture. Return to saucepan; bring to a boil, whisking constantly. Boil 1 minute, whisking constantly. Remove from heat and whisk in vanilla. Pour into a small container and cover surface with a piece of buttered plastic wrap. Refrigerate when cool.

Almond Pastry Cream

1. Beat butter with electric mixer until soft and creamy. Add almond meal, then sugar, then egg yolk, beating well after each addition. Flavor with rum and almond extract.

2. Beat in Pastry Cream. Place in metal bowl and freeze until very firm.

A bowl full of Ice Cream–Filled Profiteroles topped with a velvety smooth Bittersweet Chocolate Sauce is a dessert that is simply irresistible. See page 105.

Cream Puff Pastry

Cream puff pastry, unlike puff pastry, is quite easy to prepare; it is not something that should only be attempted by aspiring pastry chefs. It is a delicious pastry that can be used in a multitude of ways, acting as a simple and delicate foil to an array of sweet fillings. Whipped cream, custards, and pastry cream acquire a more delightful and elegant character when paired with cream puff pastry. Éclairs, profiteroles, and Paris-Brest are just a few of the cream puff pastry creations featured here.

CREAM PUFF PASTRY BASICS

Cream puff pastry is the dough used to make cream puffs, éclairs, profiteroles, swans, Paris-Brest, Gâteau Saint-Honoré, and croquembouche. It is quickly and simply made from a paste of water, butter, salt, sugar, and flour to which eggs are added one by one, causing the pastry to inflate like a balloon in the oven and form a crisp, puffy shell that can be filled with a variety of creams and glazed with different icings. The usual fillings are pastry cream, Chantilly cream, ice cream, or mousse. The toppings range from a dusting of confectioners' sugar to a rich chocolate glaze or crunchy caramel topping.

The basic dough for cream puff pastry is easy to make and form into various shapes and sizes. The most efficient way to create precise shapes with cream puff pastry is to pipe them onto baking sheets using a pastry bag fitted with the recommended tube. See page 20 for instructions for assembling and using a pastry bag and tubes. If a pastry bag is not available, it is possible to use spoons and your fingers (dipped in egg wash or water) to roughly shape the paste.

Cream puff paste should be used while still warm. If you want to keep leftover paste, rub the surface with butter, cover, and refrigerate for up to eight hours. To use, bring to room temperature and use as you would fresh paste. Leftover paste does not puff as high as fresh paste and should be used only for small puffs, such as profiteroles or miniature éclairs.

CREAM PUFF PASTRY
Pâte à choux

For 1⅓ cups

- ½ cup water or ¼ cup water and ¼ cup milk
- 4 tablespoons unsalted butter, cut into pieces
- ¼ teaspoon salt
- ½ teaspoon sugar
- ½ cup unbleached white flour, sifted (see Note)
- 2 eggs

For 2 cups

- ¾ cup water or half water, half milk
- 6 tablespoons unsalted butter, cut into pieces
- ¼ teaspoon salt
- ¾ teaspoon sugar
- ¾ cup unbleached white flour, sifted (see Note)
- 3 eggs

For 2⅔ cups

- 1 cup water or ½ cup water and ½ cup milk
- 8 tablespoons unsalted butter cut into pieces
- ½ teaspoon salt
- 1 teaspoon sugar
- 1 cup unbleached white flour, sifted (see Note)
- 4 eggs

1. Preheat oven to 425° F. Place water, butter, salt, and sugar in a 2½-quart saucepan; bring to a boil over low heat. The mixture should be heated slowly so the butter is just melted when the water reaches a boil. When mixture boils, remove from heat immediately and add flour all at once. Stir vigorously with a wooden spoon. Return to heat; stir over medium heat until mixture pulls away from sides of pan, begins to leave a white film on pan, and forms a ball (about 30 seconds).

CREAM PUFF PASTRY YIELD	
Amount of Cream Puff Pastry	Yields:
1⅓ cups	8 éclairs
	10 cream puffs
	40 profiteroles
	1 eight-inch Paris-Brest
2 cups	12 éclairs
	15 cream puffs
	60 profiteroles
	1 nine-inch Paris-Brest
	1 nine-inch Gâteau Saint-Honoré

2. Remove from heat; allow to cool 5 minutes. Add eggs, one at a time, beating thoroughly after each addition. The paste should look smooth and shiny but be stiff enough to hold its shape when piped or dropped onto a baking sheet. If paste looks dull and is very stiff, lightly beat another egg and add a little of it to paste; beat until mixture is smooth. Add more egg if needed.

3. Pipe or spoon cream puff pastry onto parchment-lined baking sheets into shapes as specified in individual recipes. Bake as directed.

For yield, see chart above.

<u>Note</u> Unbleached white bread (hard) flour is best for making cream puff paste. All-purpose flour may be substituted if hard flour is unavailable.

SUCCESS WITH CREAM PUFF PASTRY

For well-risen pastry:

☐ Allow flour, butter, and water mixture (panada) to cool slightly before you beat in eggs. Eggs added to a scalding hot mixture could lose their leavening power.

☐ Do not add too much egg. Pastry that is runny will have thin, weak walls that collapse easily.

☐ Preheat oven. Check the oven temperature with a thermometer. Do not handle pastry or remove from oven until it has risen fully and set. Do not open and close oven door.

To produce crisp shells:

☐ If the water in the panada mixture is allowed to boil away, the ratio of water to butter changes and the resulting pastry will be greasy, making it difficult to incorporate the eggs into the dough.

☐ If the inner, uncooked dough is left in the baked pastry, its moisture will spread to the outer shell.

☐ Use cream puff pastry on the same day it is baked. Wrap loosely in plastic wrap (when cool) until ready to fill. Wrap and freeze any pastry you can't use the day it is baked. Heat frozen shells before filling in a 400° F oven 5 to 10 minutes or until crisp.

☐ Fill pastries no more than two hours before serving. Icing may be applied up to five hours in advance. Fillings can be made in advance and refrigerated. Once shells are filled with cream, they must be refrigerated to avoid spoilage. Shells quickly lose their crispness in the refrigerator, however, so it is best to store unfilled pastry shells at room temperature and fill them as close to serving time as possible.

HOW TO MAKE CREAM PUFF PASTRY

Use these step-by-step instructions, together with the tips for success at left, to create delicate, well-risen cream puff pastry every time.

1. *Place water, butter, salt, and sugar in a saucepan; bring to a boil. When mixture boils, remove from heat immediately and stir in flour all at once. Return to heat and stir vigorously with a wooden spoon over medium heat until mixture pulls away from sides of pan and forms a ball, leaving a white film on pan.*

2. *Remove from heat; cool 5 minutes. Add eggs, one at a time, beating after each addition until smooth. This photo shows how paste looks just after an egg has been added. Notice how paste separates into several lumps after the addition of an egg. When stirred vigorously the paste will return to a smooth consistency.*

3. *Cream puff pastry is ready to be piped or spooned onto a baking sheet when it reaches this smooth, shiny consistency. It should still be stiff enough to hold its shape when piped.*

4. *Fit pastry bag with a ¾-inch plain ornamenting tube. Fill bag half full with cream puff pastry. To form éclairs, pipe 5-inch strips of paste 2 inches apart on a parchment-lined baking sheet (see Éclairs, pages 102–103). To form cream puffs, pipe 2½-inch mounds of paste 2 inches apart on baking sheet (see Cream Puffs, page 105).*

PASTRY CREAM
Crème patissière

Pastry cream is a delicious, multipurpose custard (or pudding). It can be flavored and used by itself, or flavored and lightened with whipped cream or beaten egg whites. It is used as a filling for cream puff pastries, puff pastries, and cakes, and is also used in fresh fruit tarts. In some recipes, pastry cream is a base for a more complex mixture, such as the Almond Pastry Cream filling for Pithiviers (see page 97). Pastry cream can even be eaten by itself, as a vanilla pudding.

Pastry cream can be frozen successfully if either the flour or cornstarch is increased slightly to create a thicker cream. Thin pastry creams tend to separate when frozen.

For 1¼ cups

- *1 cup milk*
- *3 egg yolks*
- *¼ cup sugar*
- *2 tablespoons flour, sifted*
- *1 tablespoon cornstarch, sifted*
- *1 teaspoon vanilla extract*

For 1½ cups

- *1¼ cups milk*
- *4 egg yolks*
- *⅓ cup sugar*
- *3 tablespoons flour, sifted*
- *1 tablespoon cornstarch, sifted*
- *1 teaspoon vanilla extract*

For 2½ cups

- *2 cups milk*
- *6 egg yolks*
- *½ cup sugar*
- *¼ cup flour, sifted*
- *2 tablespoons cornstarch, sifted*
- *1½ teaspoons vanilla extract*

1. Bring milk to a boil in a medium saucepan; remove from heat.

2. In a medium bowl beat egg yolks with sugar until thick and pale. Beat in flour and cornstarch.

FLAVORINGS FOR PASTRY CREAM

Amount of Pastry Cream	Semisweet Chocolate	Dry Instant Coffee	Liqueur	Finely Ground Praline
1¼ cups	2 oz (melted and cooled)	2 tsp (dissolved in 1 tbsp boiling water)	1 tbsp	3 tbsp
1½ cups	2½ oz (melted and cooled)	2½ tsp (dissolved in 1 tbsp boiling water)	1½ tbsp	¼ cup
2½ cups	3 to 4 oz (melted and cooled)	4 tsp (dissolved in 1½ tbsp boiling water)	2 tbsp	⅓ cup

See the chart on page 22 for flavor pairings.

---

3. Pour hot milk into yolk mixture and whisk. Return to saucepan; cook over medium heat, whisking constantly, until mixture comes to a boil. Just before mixture begins to boil, it will become very lumpy. Whisk vigorously until smooth; continue to cook gently for 2 minutes, whisking constantly. (The mixture will thin slightly during this time.) Remove from heat and pour into a bowl; stir in vanilla and rub a piece of cold butter gently over the surface of the cream to prevent a skin from forming.

4. Pastry cream may be flavored when it has cooled slightly (see Flavorings for Pastry Cream, above). When pastry cream is cool, cover and refrigerate. Will keep up to 2 days in refrigerator.

Note If pastry cream is lumpy or slightly scorched, you can press it through a strainer to remove lumps and bits of brown cream. Never use cream that has a burned taste.

CHOCOLATE ÉCLAIRS

Éclairs are fingers of cream puff pastry filled with a flavored pastry cream, such as chocolate, praline, or coffee, and iced with a thin, shiny glaze. Several delicious variations follow this recipe.

- *1⅓ cups Cream Puff Pastry (see page 100)*
- *1 egg lightly beaten with 1 teaspoon water (egg wash)*
- *1½ cups Pastry Cream (see at left)*
- *½ cup whipping cream*
- *1 cup Bittersweet Chocolate Sauce (see page 105)*

1. Preheat oven to 425° F. Place Cream Puff Pastry in a large pastry bag fitted with a ¾-inch tube (no 9; see page 20). Cut a piece of parchment paper to fit a baking sheet; using a dark pen or pencil, draw two parallel lines on it 5 inches apart (parallel to the long edge of the paper) and turn paper over on baking sheet.

2. To form éclairs, pipe eight 5-inch strips of pastry, 2 inches apart, onto the paper on the baking sheet, using the lines on the paper as a guide. Brush the éclairs with egg wash. Run the back of a fork along the top of each éclair to score top and keep it flat during baking.

3. Bake at 425° F for 15 minutes. Reduce oven to 400° F and bake 15 minutes more. Make a few small slits along the side of each éclair to release steam. Turn off oven; return éclairs to oven for 10 minutes, keeping oven door slightly ajar with a wooden spoon. Cool on wire racks.

4. Prepare Pastry Cream and flavor it as desired. Stir cold Pastry Cream until smooth. Beat whipping cream until it holds stiff peaks and fold into Pastry Cream.

5. Just before serving (no more than 2 hours before), place filling in a pastry bag fitted with a ¼-inch tube (no 3). Poke a hole in one end of éclair with the tip and fill with 3 to 4 tablespoons of the filling. If you don't have a pastry bag, slit éclairs along one side with a serrated knife and spoon filling inside before icing.

6. To ice éclairs, spread 1 to 2 tablespoons warm (90° F) Bittersweet Chocolate Sauce on top of each éclair (or dip top of each in warm icing). If you want to do as much in advance as possible, you can ice the éclairs before filling them, up to 4 or 5 hours before serving. Store iced éclairs in a cool, dry place, then fill them carefully just before serving.

Makes 8 éclairs.

Éclair Variations

Double Chocolate Éclairs Fill with Pastry Cream flavored with chocolate. You can also add praline or any of the liqueurs that go with chocolate (see page 102) to the chocolate pastry cream. Glaze with Bittersweet Chocolate Sauce (see page 105) or Quick Fondant flavored with chocolate (see page 104).

Coffee Éclairs Fill with Pastry Cream flavored with coffee. Glaze éclairs with Quick Fondant (see page 104) flavored with coffee or chocolate.

Mocha Éclairs Fill with Pastry Cream flavored with coffee and chocolate (to make mocha). Glaze with Quick Fondant flavored with coffee or chocolate (see page 104) or Bittersweet Chocolate Sauce (see page 105).

Caramel Éclairs Dip éclairs in caramel (see page 24); cool upside down on a cold baking sheet. Fill with vanilla or praline-flavored Pastry Cream.

Chocolate Éclairs are favorites of most everyone. Cream puff pastry is filled with vanilla pastry cream and iced with Bittersweet Chocolate Sauce. The flavor of the pastry cream can be varied easily. Refer to the chart on opposite page.

FONDANT ICING

Fondant icing is shiny and soft, but when set its surface forms a thin crust, making it easy to handle. It is commonly used to ice éclairs, petits fours, and other miniature pastries. Fondant can be flavored with melted chocolate, instant coffee, or liqueur. White fondant may be tinted to pastel shades with a few drops of red or green food coloring. You can buy regular fondant by the pound in specialty food stores or bakeries, or you can make your own Quick Fondant.

QUICK FONDANT

- 1½ cups confectioners' sugar
- 1 to 2 tablespoons water

1. Sift sugar into a bowl. Stir in water until icing is a spreadable consistency.

2. Flavor with 1 ounce melted chocolate, ½ teaspoon instant coffee dissolved in 1 teaspoon hot water, or liqueur to taste. Remember that some flavorings will make the icing more liquid. Place icing over hot water and heat to lukewarm (110° F). Spread on éclairs while warm. If icing is too thick, thin with a little warm water. If too thin, add a little sifted confectioners' sugar.

Makes 1 cup.

PARIS-BREST

Some speculate that the ring-shaped cake called Paris-Brest takes its name from a celebrated bicycle race between Paris and Brest. Others claim that it was a cake that could be prepared quickly for the diners on the train between Paris and Brest. Paris-Brest is a large cream puff ring filled with a light praline-flavored cream called *crème chiboust*. You can make the cream puff ring, pastry cream, and praline in advance. Reheat pastry cream and fill cake just before serving. If all of the parts are ready, the cake takes no more than 10 minutes to assemble.

- 2 cups Cream Puff Pastry (see page 100)
- 1 egg lightly beaten with 1 teaspoon water (egg wash)
- ⅓ cup sliced blanched almonds
- 2 teaspoons unflavored gelatin
- 1 tablespoon dark rum mixed with 1 tablespoon water
- 1½ cups Pastry Cream (see page 102)
- 4 egg whites
- ¼ cup sugar
- ¼ cup finely ground praline (see page 24)
- 2 tablespoons confectioners' sugar

1. Preheat oven to 425° F. Using a dark pen or pencil, trace a 9-inch circle on a piece of parchment paper. Turn paper over and place on baking sheet. Place fresh Cream Puff Pastry in a pastry bag fitted with a ¾-inch tube (no 9). Pipe a circle of the pastry on the line you've drawn. Pipe a second circle just inside it, so it touches the first circle. Pipe a third circle centered on top of the lower two. Brush the surface of the pastry with egg wash and sprinkle with sliced almonds.

2. Bake in preheated oven until puffed and light brown (20 minutes). Reduce oven to 400° F and bake until golden brown and completely set (20 to 30 minutes longer). Poke several slits around sides of cake; turn oven off; keep door of oven ajar about ½ inch with wooden spoon, and allow cake to dry out in oven for 15 minutes or until very crisp.

3. Cool on wire cooling rack. Preheat oven to 375° F. Using a serrated knife, slice off the top third of the cake, and scoop out any uncooked dough. Place top and bottom, brown side down, on a baking sheet. Return to oven for 5 to 10 minutes to dry out inside. Cool before filling.

4. *To fill Paris-Brest:* Soften gelatin in rum and water; set aside until spongy.

5. Prepare Pastry Cream. While Pastry Cream is hot, stir in softened gelatin. Whisk vigorously to dissolve gelatin in hot cream.

6. Beat egg whites until stiff but not dry. Gradually beat in sugar and continue beating until stiff and glossy.

7. Stir Praline and one fourth of whites into hot Pastry Cream. Gently fold in the remaining whites. Place bottom of Paris-Brest on serving platter. Place cream in a large pastry bag fitted with a large open-star tip (no 9). Pipe the cream decoratively into the bottom half of the cake using a shell or rosette pattern. If you don't have a pastry bag, spoon cream into the cake. Pipe another layer of cream on top of the first. Carefully place top of Paris-Brest on filling. Sift confectioners' sugar over cake.

8. Serve within 1 hour of assembly. If not served immediately, cover and refrigerate.

Serves 8.

ICE CREAM–FILLED PROFITEROLES WITH BITTERSWEET CHOCOLATE SAUCE

Imagine a mound of tiny cream puffs filled with your favorite ice cream and covered with warm Bittersweet Chocolate Sauce.

- 1⅓ cups Cream Puff Pastry (see page 100)
- 1 egg lightly beaten with 1 teaspoon water (egg wash)
- 1 pint vanilla or coffee ice cream

Bittersweet Chocolate Sauce

- 3 tablespoons water
- 3 tablespoons sugar
- 6 ounces semisweet chocolate, broken into pieces
- 2 ounces unsweetened chocolate, broken into pieces
- 1 cup whipping cream

1. Preheat oven to 425° F. Line baking sheets with parchment paper. Attach parchment to baking sheet at corners with dots of Cream Puff Pastry. Place Cream Puff Pastry in a pastry bag fitted with a ½-inch tube (no 6). Pipe 48 one-inch-diameter mounds of pastry onto paper-lined baking sheets (at least ½ inch apart). Brush each puff with egg wash, while flattening the top slightly.

2. Bake for 10 minutes. Reduce oven to 400° F and bake until crisp and brown (about 10 minutes longer). Poke a ⅛-inch hole in bottom of each puff with tip of knife or tiny pastry tube. Turn off oven; return to oven until dried out (5 to 10 minutes). Prop oven door slightly ajar with a wooden spoon. Cool on wire racks.

3. *To fill pastries:* Place a baking sheet in freezer. Slice each puff in half horizontally. Form 48 tiny mounds (1 rounded teaspoon each) of ice cream on the sheet.

Flash-freeze. Cover ice cream mounds and store in freezer until ready to fill profiteroles. Before serving, fill bottom half of each shell with one of the ice cream mounds, then put top half of shell on top. Place 6 to 8 filled profiteroles in each dessert bowl. Pour about 3 tablespoons warm Bittersweet Chocolate Sauce over puffs. Serve immediately.

Makes 8 servings, 6 puffs each.

Bittersweet Chocolate Sauce

Here's a sauce that is everything a chocolate sauce should be. It flows easily when warm, coating with a thin, bittersweet chocolate glaze. This sauce is thick enough to use as an icing on top of éclairs. Cool to 90° F and spread 1 to 2 tablespoons on top of each éclair.

1. Combine water and sugar in a saucepan; bring to a boil over low heat, stirring constantly until sugar dissolves. Remove from heat and cool to 120° F (test with an instant-read thermometer).

2. Combine semisweet and unsweetened chocolate in top of double boiler; place over hot (not boiling) water until chocolate is just melted. Remove from heat. Pour in sugar syrup (at 120° F) all at once. Stir until smooth.

3. Heat cream in a small saucepan over low heat to 120° F. Pour into chocolate mixture and stir until smooth and shiny.

Makes 2 cups.

Vanilla Pastry Cream–Filled Profiteroles

Prepare profiteroles, following steps 1 and 2 above; do not slice in half. Prepare 1 cup Pastry Cream (see page 102), flavored with vanilla and lightened with ½ cup stiffly whipped cream. Place the cream in a small pastry bag fitted with a ⅛-inch tube, and fill pastries through the hole in the bottom of each puff. Fill as close to serving time as possible.

CREAM PUFFS

Cream puffs can be filled with Chantilly Cream or flavored Pastry Cream. They are finished with a light dusting of confectioners' sugar. Fill no more than two hours prior to serving.

- 1⅓ cups Cream Puff Pastry (see page 100)
- 1 egg lightly beaten with 1 teaspoon water (egg wash)
- 2 cups Chantilly Cream (see page 59) or 1½ cups Pastry Cream (see page 102) folded with 1 cup Chantilly Cream
- ¼ cup confectioners' sugar

1. Preheat oven to 425° F. Line a baking sheet with a piece of parchment paper. Attach paper to baking sheet with a few dots of Cream Puff Pastry. Place Cream Puff Pastry in a pastry bag fitted with a ¾-inch tube (no 9). Pipe 2½-inch-diameter mounds of pastry about 2 inches apart on baking sheet (or drop mounds of pastry onto sheet using two spoons). Brush surface of each mound with egg wash.

2. Bake at 425° F for 15 minutes. Reduce oven to 400° F and continue baking 15 minutes longer. Make a few small slits in the side of each cream puff; turn oven off and return cream puffs to oven for 10 minutes. Prop oven door slightly ajar with a wooden spoon. Cool on wire racks.

3. *To fill cream puffs:* Slice shells in half horizontally with a serrated knife. Remove any uncooked dough from inside. Place Chantilly Cream or lightened Pastry Cream in a pastry bag fitted with a medium star tip (no 7). Pipe cream into bottom half of shell until it extends 1 inch above the rim; set top half of shell on top of the cream. Sift confectioners' sugar over filled puffs. Serve immediately or refrigerate until ready to serve.

Makes 8 to 10 large puffs.

CREAM PUFF PASTRY PETITS FOURS

Perfect for parties, holiday celebrations, or afternoon teas, cream puff pastry can be piped into three different shapes to make a fine display of petits fours: profiteroles (1-inch cream puffs), éclairs (1¼-inch fingers), and sa-lambôs (1¼-inch ovals).

All three shapes can be piped onto the same baking sheet because they all bake at the same temperature for the same amount of time. Although it looks as if you have baked three different desserts, you have really only spent the time necessary to make one.

AMOUNT OF INGREDIENTS TO MAKE MINIATURE PASTRIES

Ingredients	Number of Pastries		
	40	**60**	**80**
Cream Puff Pastry	1⅓ cups	2 cups	2⅔ cups
Filling	2 cups	3 cups	4 cups
Icing	1½ cups	2¼ cups	3 cups
Caramel	1 cup	1½ cups	2 cups

How to Make Petits Fours

Profiteroles, éclairs, and salambôs can be filled and iced in several ways to create an even greater variety that is sure to please every one of your guests. The Flavor Pairings Chart (page 22) will help you create tasty combinations of fillings and icings for your miniature cream puff pastries. Think of the basic flavor you want for the filling and consult the chart to choose an appropriate flavor for the topping. For example, pastries filled with coffee pastry cream could be topped with mocha- or coffee-flavored fondant or with chocolate sauce. Kirsch-flavored pastry cream might be best topped with plain fondant icing and toasted almonds.

Consult the chart to determine how much cream puff pastry, filling, and icing it takes to produce a certain number of miniature cream puff pastries (profiteroles, salambôs, or éclairs).

To Form and Bake:

Éclairs Using a pastry bag fitted with a ½-inch tube, pipe 1¼-inch ovals of Cream Puff Pastry onto parchment-lined baking sheets. Bake as for Ice Cream-Filled Profiteroles (see page 105).

Profiteroles Form and bake as in recipe for Ice Cream-Filled Profiteroles (see page 105).

Salambôs Using a pastry bag fitted with a ½-inch tube, pipe 1¼-inch ovals of Cream Puff Pastry onto parchment-lined baking sheets. Bake as for Ice Cream-Filled Profiteroles (see page 105).

To Fill:

Fill éclairs, profiteroles, or salambôs as for Vanilla Pastry Cream-Filled Profiteroles (see page 105). Flavor Pastry Cream as desired (see page 102) or fill with Chantilly Cream (see page 59). For caramel-dipped pastries, see Caramel, below.

To Decorate Tops:

With Icing Dip tops of filled pastries in flavored fondant icing (see page 104) or Bittersweet Chocolate Sauce (see page 105). Allow icing to set before serving.

With Icing and Nuts Dip tops of filled pastries in fondant icing (see page 104) or Bittersweet Choc-olate Sauce (see page 105) and sprin-kle with chopped, toasted nuts while icing is still warm.

With Caramel Dip unfilled pastry shells in hot caramel (see page 24) and place caramel-side down on a baking sheet. When caramel hardens, remove from baking sheet and fill as for Vanilla Pastry Cream-Filled Profiteroles (see page 105).

With Confectioners' Sugar Filled profiteroles can be dusted with a light layer of confectioners' sugar.

This red tray filled with profiteroles (a variety of cream puff pastry petits fours) makes a stunning presentation, ideal for parties.

Gâteau Saint-Honoré is made from a base of puff pastry and cream puff pastry. The center is filled with a light pastry cream.

GÂTEAU SAINT-HONORÉ

Cream puff pastry and classic puff pastry combine to form this Parisian specialty named after Saint Honoré—the patron saint of pastry cooks. Cream-filled profiteroles dipped in caramel stand in a ring around the edge of a puff pastry base. The center is filled with a rum pastry cream lightened with meringue. The crisp, buttery puff pastry, crunchy caramel-iced cream puffs, and light rum cream are a delightful combination of tastes and textures.

½ recipe Classic Puff Pastry (11 oz) with 6 turns (see page 88)
2 cups Cream Puff Pastry (see page 100)
1 egg lightly beaten with 1 teaspoon water (egg wash)
2½ cups Pastry Cream (see page 102)
¼ cup whipping cream
1½ cups sugar
½ cup water
2 teaspoons unflavored gelatin
2 tablespoons dark rum or water
4 egg whites (use whites left from Pastry Cream)
¼ cup sugar

1. *To prepare pastry:* Roll out Classic Puff Pastry ³/₁₆ inch thick; cover and refrigerate 30 minutes. Cut out a 9½-inch-diameter circle of puff pastry and place on a parchment-lined baking sheet. Prick dough all over with a fork; cover and refrigerate 30 minutes.

2. Preheat oven to 450° F. Make Cream Puff Pastry and place one third of it in a pastry bag fitted with a ¾-inch tube (no 9). Pipe a border of cream puff pastry on top of the puff pastry, around the edge. Brush cream puff pastry with egg wash; do not allow egg wash to drip down sides of puff pastry base. Place remaining cream puff pastry in a pastry bag fitted with a ½-inch tube (no 6), and pipe an open spiral of paste on top of the puff pastry base beginning at the center (the lines of the spiral should not touch one another). This keeps puff pastry weighted down so it doesn't peak in the center when baked.

3. Bake for 10 minutes. Reduce oven to 400° F and bake until cream puff pastry is puffed, brown, and crisp, and puff pastry is golden brown (20 minutes longer). Turn oven off and leave pastry in oven 10 minutes with door several inches ajar.

4. Preheat oven to 425° F. Using a ½-inch tube (no 6), pipe remaining cream puff pastry into eighteen to twenty 1-inch-diameter mounds on another parchment-lined baking sheet. Brush each with egg wash. Bake for 10 minutes. Reduce oven to 400° F and bake until puffs are crisp and brown. Poke a ⅛-inch hole in the bottom of each puff, turn oven off, and allow puffs to dry out in oven with door ajar for 10 minutes. Cool before filling.

5. *To fill puffs:* Prepare Pastry Cream. Refrigerate ½ cup of the pastry cream until cool. Set aside remaining 2 cups in a bowl. Whip the whipping cream until stiff. Fold whipped cream into the ½ cup cool pastry cream. Place mixture in a small pastry bag fitted with a ⅛-inch tube and fill puffs through small hole in the bottom.

6. *To glaze puffs:* Place the 1½ cups sugar and the water in a small, heavy saucepan. Stir over medium heat until sugar is dissolved and syrup comes to a boil. When syrup boils, allow to cook over medium heat *without stirring* until syrup reaches a medium caramel color. Remove from heat and place pan in a bowl of cold water to arrest cooking.

7. Holding them on the tip of a knife or a thin-tined fork, dip top of each puff, one by one, in the caramel and place upside down on a baking sheet to harden. Reheat caramel. Dip bottom of each puff in caramel. Place them very close to one another on top of the cream puff pastry border on the edge of the cake. These caramelized puffs will form a container to hold the pastry cream filling.

8. *To make filling:* Soften gelatin in rum and set aside until soft and spongy. Gently heat the remaining 2 cups pastry cream in a heavy saucepan or the top of double boiler until bubbly, stirring constantly. Remove from heat and dissolve the softened gelatin in the hot pastry cream; stir well.

9. Beat egg whites until they form soft peaks; add the ¼ cup sugar, 1 tablespoon at a time, and continue beating until whites are stiff and glossy. Stir one fourth of the beaten whites into the hot pastry cream. Then carefully fold in the remaining whites. Place in a large pastry bag fitted with an open-star tip (no 9) and pipe filling into center of cake in high, shell-shaped mounds.

10. Refrigerate cake until ready to serve. It is best to assemble cake just before serving. To serve, cut in wedges.

Serves 6 to 8.

A light dusting of confectioners' sugar is the finishing touch applied to delicate Madeleines. The shell-like shape comes from the mold in which they are baked.

Specialty Cookies

The wonderful, delicate textures,
flavors, and decorations of
the special cookies featured
in this chapter make them
resemble cakes and pastries much
more than the traditional
drop cookies commonly eaten as snacks.
Serve these delightful cookies
at teas and coffees in the afternoon
or at the conclusion
of a fine meal. Everyone
will love them because
they are light
and unbelievably
delicious.

COOKIES AS DESSERT

A tempting array of elegant and unusual cookies attractively displayed on a tray makes a striking dessert. Fresh fruit sorbet (see page 120), ice cream, and frozen soufflés are the perfect companions for these bite-sized delicacies.

Not only do these cookies taste wonderful, they have a distinctive look as well. Simple tricks for shaping and decorating give these cookies a uniquely professional look that sets them apart from everyday fare. People might not believe you made them yourself. These cookies are too pretty to be casually dumped into a cookie jar and eaten Cookie-Monster style at midnight. Arrange them on a cookie platter or silver tray to show off their elegance.

You may want to prepare other types of miniature pastries to mix in with the cookies. Tiny tartlets (filled with lemon and fresh fruit), tiny cream puffs (profiteroles, salambôs, éclairs), or chocolate-dipped strawberries are examples of fresh petits fours that go well with cookies and add color to a cookie display.

COOKIE-BAKING EQUIPMENT

The single most important piece of equipment for baking cookies is a good baking sheet. Invest in a few heavy-gauge metal baking sheets. A heavy-gauge metal pan has even heat distribution and will not buckle when placed in a hot oven. Shiny metal pans that will dull and darken with use are preferable. Avoid heavy, black metal pans because they hold heat, causing cookies to burn more easily.

Nonstick baking sheets are useful, but most nonstick sheets made for household use are too thin. Always regrease or reline baking sheets with kitchen parchment between batches. When lining baking sheets with silicone-treated parchment paper, cut parchment to exact inside dimensions of baking sheet. For more information on cookie-baking equipment, see page 9.

CURRANT BUTTER THINS
Palets de dames

It's easy to eat dozens of these tiny butter thins. Currants provide a simple and delicious decoration.

- ¼ cup dried currants
- 7 tablespoons unsalted butter, softened
- ½ cup sugar
- 2 fresh egg whites, lightly beaten
- ½ teaspoon vanilla extract
- ⅔ cup flour, sifted with a pinch of salt

1. Preheat oven to 400° F. Lightly butter baking sheets.

2. Cover currants with boiling water; allow to stand 10 minutes; drain well. Dry on paper towels.

3. In medium bowl of electric mixer, cream butter and sugar until light. Gradually beat in egg whites. Stir in vanilla and flour.

4. Place batter in a small pastry bag fitted with a ¼-inch tube (no 3). Pipe 1-inch-diameter rounds 1 inch apart onto baking sheets. Use a spoon to form the rounds if you don't have a pastry bag. Place 3 currants on top of each cookie. Bake until ¼ inch of edge is brown but center is still pale (8 to 10 minutes). Cool on wire racks.

5. Store in airtight container for up to 2 weeks. For variety, these cookies can be brushed with melted and sieved warm apricot jam just before serving.

Makes 9 dozen cookies.

FINANCIERS
Almond tartlets

When served minutes after baking, these delectable French almond tartlets have a crisp, buttery edge and chewy almond center.

Use individual miniature tartlet tins or muffin tins with a 1-tablespoon capacity. These tins can be round, oval, boat shaped, square, diamond shaped, and so forth, with plain or fluted sides.

- 3 fresh egg whites
- 1½ cups sifted confectioners' sugar
- ¾ cup finely ground blanched almonds (see page 67)
- ⅓ cup flour, sifted
- 7 tablespoons unsalted butter, melted and cooled
- 2 tablespoons sliced almonds, for decoration

1. Preheat oven to 450° F. Brush inside of each tin (1-tablespoon capacity) with melted butter and place tins on a baking sheet. If you do not have enough tins, bake tartlets one batch at a time. Allow tins to cool between batches; brush tins again with melted butter and bake next batch in preheated oven.

2. In a medium bowl beat egg whites until foamy. Beat in confectioners' sugar, ground almonds, and flour one after another; beat until just mixed. Stir in melted butter.

3. Spoon ½ tablespoon batter into each tin (or fill half full). Place one almond slice on each tartlet.

4. Bake 5 minutes on center rack in oven. Reduce oven to 400° F and bake 5 minutes more. Check cookies frequently because they can burn quickly. Turn off oven and leave cookies in oven 5 minutes. Remove from oven when brown and unmold immediately while still warm. These cookies have a tendency to stick to tins when cool; use tip of sharp knife to help unmold.

Makes 42 to 48 cookies.

CHOCOLATE-DIPPED ALMOND MERINGUE BATONS

Little almond-covered meringue batons are filled with almond paste and dipped in chocolate. These attractive cookies are sure to be a favorite.

> 1 cup plus 2 tablespoons finely ground blanched almonds (4 oz) (see page 67)
> ⅔ cup sugar
> ¼ cup flour, sifted
> 5 egg whites
> 2 tablespoons sugar
> 1¼ cups chopped blanched almonds (4½ oz)
> 1 teaspoon kirsch
> 2 ounces almond paste or marzipan (see page 28)
> 6 to 8 ounces semisweet chocolate (couverture is best, see page 32)

1. Preheat oven to 350° F. Line baking sheets with parchment paper cut to fit sheet exactly.

2. Place ground almonds and the ⅔ cup sugar in bowl of food processor fitted with steel blade. Process until ground to a fine powder (about 10 seconds). Do not overprocess or mixture will turn to almond paste. Sift flour over this mixture and blend briefly in food processor or by hand.

3. *To make meringue:* In a large bowl beat egg whites until they hold peaks. Add the 2 tablespoons sugar and continue beating until stiff and glossy. Gently fold almond mixture into the whites until fully incorporated but not deflated. Place this meringue in a large pastry bag fitted with a ½-inch tube (no 6). Pipe 2½-inch batons (finger shapes) about ½ inch apart on parchment-lined baking sheets. Scatter chopped almonds liberally over the cookies so each cookie is covered with chopped almonds.

4. Bake until cookies are light brown all over (20 to 25 minutes). Cool on baking sheets. When cookies are cool and crisp, carefully remove from parchment and store in an airtight container until ready to assemble.

5. *To assemble cookies:* Mix kirsch into almond paste with a fork. Work this mixture until it is spreadable. Spread about ⅛ teaspoon almond paste mixture on the center of the flat side (bottom) of half of the cookies. Make little sandwiches by placing another cookie on top of each (flat side toward center). Melt and temper chocolate (see page 32). When chocolate is 86° F to 90° F, dip both ends of each baton into the chocolate (chocolate should cover ¼ inch to ½ inch of each end). It is best to assemble cookies on the day they are to be served.

Makes 4 dozen cookies.

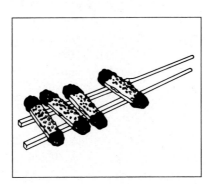

TIP FOR COOLING CHOCOLATE-DIPPED COOKIES Set pairs of chopsticks or skewers ¾ inch apart on counter or baking sheets. Set each chocolate-dipped cookie on the chopsticks so the chocolate ends are suspended and can dry without touching anything.

Tips

SUCCESSFUL COOKIE BAKING

☐ Several recipes call for fresh egg whites. Use only whites from freshly cracked eggs. Do not use egg whites that have been stored in refrigerator or freezer.

☐ Bake only on center rack of oven. Allow at least 1 inch of space between baking sheets and walls of the oven.

☐ Check cookies to make sure they are browning evenly. Turn the baking sheet if necessary to adjust for hot spots in the oven.

☐ Check cookies before the recommended baking time is up to see if they are browning more quickly than expected.

☐ Cool cookies completely before storing. Store between sheets of parchment paper in an airtight container, in a cool, dry place.

☐ Although filled cookies will keep one week, they are best if assembled on the day they are to be eaten.

☐ Most cookies can be frozen successfully. However, chocolate-dipped or decorated cookies may not look as attractive after freezing.

☐ It is best to freeze the cookies before dipping or decorating them. Thaw and recrisp cookies, then decorate or dip.

☐ The length of time that cookies can be frozen depends on the type of freezer you have and the temperature it maintains.

HOW TO MAKE ALMOND TUILES

1. *Place 1 tablespoon of batter every 4 inches on parchment-lined baking sheets. Use the back of a fork to flatten each mound into a 3-inch round, so almonds are well spread out in a single layer.*

2. *Bake one sheet of cookies at a time because cookies cool quickly and must be molded into a U shape while still warm. Remove baked cookies one at a time from parchment with a thin metal spatula. Immediately place top side down in metal baguette pans or top side up over a narrow rolling pin. Remove from mold when cookies are cool and crisp. If flat cookies harden before you have a chance to shape them, return to oven until warm and pliable.*

ALMOND TUILES

Have a cookie-baking party with your friends to make these U-shaped almond crisps and others. Use a wooden dowel or similarly shaped object to form the U shape after baking.

- ⅔ cup sugar
- 3 egg whites
- 6 tablespoons flour, sifted
- 3 tablespoons unsalted butter, melted and cooled
- 2 cups sliced blanched or natural almonds
- ½ teaspoon finely grated lemon rind
- ½ teaspoon vanilla extract

1. Preheat oven to 350° F. In a large bowl whisk sugar into egg whites all at once; continue whisking for 1 minute. Stir in flour, butter, almonds, lemon rind, and vanilla.

2. Line baking sheets with lightly buttered parchment paper. Place a tablespoon of batter every 4 inches on parchment-lined baking sheets. Flatten each mound with the tines of a dinner fork into a 3-inch round that is 1/16 inch thick (almonds should be well spread out in one layer). Bake only one sheet of cookies at a time because they cool quickly and must be shaped while still warm.

3. Bake until light brown all over (10 to 12 minutes). Meanwhile, butter wooden dowels (1½ to 2 inches in diameter) or narrow metal baguette pans. Remove cookies from oven and allow to cool 5 seconds. Remove cookies from parchment one at a time using a narrow metal spatula. Place top side up over a buttered dowel or top side down in baguette pans. Either method will create a U-shaped cookie that resembles an open taco shell. If cookies harden on baking sheet, return them to oven until they soften and are flexible enough to bend easily.

4. When cookies are completely cool and crisp, carefully transfer to an airtight container. They keep several days in dry weather but have a tendency to absorb moisture and grow limp in wet weather. They are best when served just after baking. Serve rounded side up. Delicious with ice cream or sorbet.

Makes 30 cookies.

FLORENTINES

Crisp orange-and-almond lace cookies are glazed with bittersweet chocolate to make an irresistible cookie.

- 3 tablespoons unsalted butter, softened
- ½ cup whipping cream
- ⅔ cup sugar
- 1 cup very finely chopped candied orange rind (scant) (see page 31)
- 1½ cups blanched almonds, finely chopped
- ½ cup sliced blanched almonds
- ⅓ cup flour, sifted
- 8 ounces semisweet or bittersweet chocolate (couverture is best, see page 32)

1. Preheat oven to 350° F. Line baking sheets with buttered and floured parchment paper.

2. In a 2½-quart saucepan bring the butter, cream, and sugar to a boil over medium heat, stirring frequently.

3. Remove from heat and stir in candied orange rind and chopped and sliced almonds. Stir in flour.

4. Place teaspoonfuls of batter about 3 inches apart on prepared baking sheets. Flatten each cookie with a fork dipped in water.

5. Bake 6 minutes. Remove from oven and pull in the edges of each cookie with a 2½-inch round cookie cutter. This will help the cookie to bake in a round shape. Return to the oven and bake until light brown (5 to 7 minutes longer). Slide parchment onto a wire rack and allow cookies to cool before removing them from the paper.

6. Melt and temper chocolate (see page 32). When chocolate is 86° F, spread a thin layer of chocolate on the flat side (bottom) of each cookie. When the chocolate on the cookie is almost set, mark it with wavy lines, using a cake-decorating comb or a fork. Place in the refrigerator for 10 minutes or until the chocolate is just set.

Makes 54 cookies.

Note These cookies will soften and grow sticky if stored in a moist place or made during rainy weather.

CIGARETTES RUSSES

Thin, buttery wafers are baked until golden brown and then rolled into cigarette or cone shapes.

> ½ cup unsalted butter, softened
> 1 cup confectioner's sugar, sifted
> 4 medium fresh egg whites
> ⅔ cup flour
> ½ teaspoon vanilla extract
> 3 ounces semisweet chocolate, melted (optional)

1. In medium bowl of electric mixer, cream butter; add sugar and beat until light.

2. Beat in egg whites one by one.

3. Stir in flour just until mixed. Stir in vanilla.

4. Preheat oven to 375° F. Place a small amount of batter in a pastry bag fitted with a ¼-inch tube tip. Pipe out one test cookie and bake (see steps 5 and 6). If the baked cookie is thick and chewy rather than thin, flat, and crisp, thin the batter with 1 tablespoon melted butter.

5. Lightly butter some parchment paper and line baking sheets with it. Place batter in pastry bag. If you do not have a pastry bag, drop a tablespoonful of batter onto baking sheet for each cookie.

6. Pipe 1½-inch-diameter mounds of batter about 3 inches apart on baking sheets. Rap baking sheet on counter a couple of times to spread batter slightly. Bake only one sheet of cookies at a time because cookies cool quickly and must be shaped while warm. Bake until brown around edges (8 to 10 minutes).

7. Remove cookies one by one from baking sheet while still warm and pliable. Roll each cookie around the buttered handle of a wooden spoon. To form a cone shape, wrap around a metal or wooden cone. Cool cookies on wire racks.

8. These cookies may be served plain or ends of cookies can be dipped in melted chocolate. They are best when consumed immediately after baking, but will keep in an airtight container in a dry place for 2 to 3 days.

Makes 3 dozen cookies.

Step-by-step

HOW TO MAKE CIGARETTES RUSSES

1. Baking sheet in rear shows batter being piped in 1½-inch mounds about 3 inches apart on parchment-lined baking sheets. Baking sheet in front shows piped mounds as they look after baking sheet has been rapped firmly on counter a couple of times to spread batter slightly. Cookies are now ready for baking.

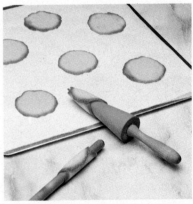

2. Bake only one sheet of cookies at a time. Remove baked cookies one by one from baking sheet while still warm and pliable. Roll each cookie around a buttered wooden spoon or cone to shape. Remove from mold when cool and crisp. If flat cookies harden too quickly before you have a chance to shape them, return them to oven until warm and pliable.

These two types of cookies, the long, thin Sacristans and the bell-shaped Palmiers, are made from Classic Puff Pastry (see page 88). The Palmiers are sprinkled with sugar before baking, while the Sacristans are rolled in crystallized sugar and chopped almonds.

PALMIERS
Palm leaves

Crisp, caramelized palmiers are made from Classic Puff Pastry that has been rolled out in sugar (rather than flour) for its last two turns (turns 5 and 6).

> 1 recipe Classic Puff Pastry (21 oz) with 4 turns (see page 88)
> 1½ cups sugar

1. Sprinkle work surface and surface of Classic Puff Pastry with sugar; give dough a fifth turn (see page 88). Repeat for sixth turn. Cut puff pastry in half. Wrap dough and chill until dough has relaxed enough to roll out easily (about 1 hour).

2. Remove one piece of pastry from refrigerator. Sprinkle work surface and dough with sugar and roll out into an 8- by 18-inch rectangle, ⅛ inch thick. Cover and chill until firm (10 minutes in freezer). Trim to make a rectangle with parallel sides. Mark the center on the 8-inch sides; fold dough lengthwise in toward center mark so the edges barely meet; press down on top layer of dough with fingers. Brush top lightly with water, then fold dough in half lengthwise to form a long, narrow bar that is 2 inches wide and 18 inches long. This bar now has 4 layers of dough. Press down on dough again, wrap, and place in freezer until firm enough to cut easily. Repeat folding process with other piece of puff pastry.

3. Preheat oven to 400° F. Line baking sheets with parchment or use nonstick sheets. With a sharp knife slice dough into ¼-inch slices. Place slices cut edge down on baking sheet about 2 inches apart. Spread the two loose ends of each slice slightly and shape to resemble a bell. Flatten each slightly. Place in freezer 20 minutes.

4. Bake on middle rack of oven, one sheet at a time, for 15 minutes. Lower oven temperature to 350° F. Turn each cookie over with metal spatula. Continue baking until caramelized and golden brown on both sides (15 to 20 minutes). Watch carefully to avoid burning. If browning too quickly, lower oven temperature to 325° F. Preheat oven to 400° F for each batch of cookies.

5. Cool on wire racks. Store in airtight container for up to 1 week. Can be frozen and recrisped in oven for 5 to 10 minutes at 350° F.
Makes about 10 dozen 2-inch cookies.

MADELEINES

Browned butter adds a delicate nutty flavor and aroma to these airy, shell-shaped sponge cookies.

½ cup unsalted butter
2 eggs
½ cup sugar
1 teaspoon finely grated lemon rind
¼ teaspoon lemon juice
¼ teaspoon vanilla extract
⅛ teaspoon baking powder
¾ cup sifted cake flour

1. Melt butter in a saucepan over medium heat until the milk solids in the butter turn a golden brown color (this will occur just after the foam subsides). Transfer to a small stainless steel bowl and allow to cool 10 minutes.

2. Place eggs and sugar in a medium stainless steel bowl and whisk over boiling water until mixture is tepid (98° F). Remove from heat and whisk in lemon rind, lemon juice, and vanilla. Sift baking powder and flour together; stir into egg mixture. Stir in melted and cooled butter. Cover bowl with plastic wrap and allow to rest 1 hour at room temperature.

3. Preheat oven to 450° F. Brush inside of madeleine pans (inside the shells) with thin layer of melted butter. Dust with flour, then invert pan and rap briskly on counter to remove excess flour. Spoon batter into shells, filling each shell three-fourths full.

4. Bake small (1½-inch) madeleines until cookies rise in center and are very light brown on the bottom and edges (3 to 4 minutes). When done, they will spring back when lightly touched in the center. Remove madeleines from oven, invert pan over wire cooling rack, and tap lightly to release cookies from pan. Bake 3-inch madeleines 10 to 12 minutes.

5. Cookies are best when served immediately, while still warm. Otherwise, cool completely and store in an airtight container or freeze until ready to use.

Makes 40 small madeleines or 15 large madeleines.

SACRISTANS

These almond sugar twists are delicate, crunchy, and full-flavored. Made from Classic Puff Pastry, they have a different texture from most cookies. You'll be tempted to eat the whole batch.

1 recipe Classic Puff Pastry (21 oz) with 4 turns (see page 88)
1 cup crystal sugar or raw sugar (see below)
1 cup finely chopped blanched almonds
1 egg, lightly beaten with 1 teaspoon water (egg wash)

1. Cut Classic Puff Pastry in half. Roll each half out into an 8- by 18-inch rectangle, ⅛ inch thick. Cover and chill 15 minutes.

2. Combine crystal sugar and almonds. Remove one rectangle of puff pastry from refrigerator, brush one side of it with egg wash and sprinkle with ½ cup of sugar/almond mixture. Press sugar/almond mixture into dough by rolling over it with a rolling pin. Turn dough over and repeat as for first side. Place sheet of dough on a parchment-lined baking sheet, cover with plastic wrap, and chill in freezer until dough is firm enough to cut easily. Repeat with second rectangle of puff pastry.

3. When sheets of dough are firm, remove one sheet from freezer. With a long, sharp knife or pastry-cutting wheel, cut it in half lengthwise. Then cut the two long bands of dough crosswise into ¾-inch strips. Each strip will be ¾ inch wide and 4 inches long and will form one cookie. Line 4 baking sheets with parchment paper.

4. Twist each strip of dough twice and place on baking sheet, pressing the ends of each strip onto the paper. (This keeps the cookie in place and helps to keep it from untwisting during baking.) Cover and refrigerate 1 hour. Repeat this process with remaining sheet of puff pastry. Cookies may be frozen at this point.

5. Preheat oven to 400° F. Bake cookies, one sheet at a time, on middle rack of oven 15 minutes; turn cookies over with a metal spatula. Lower oven temperature to 325° F and continue baking until cookies are golden brown (15 to 20 minutes). Cool on wire rack. Store in an airtight container up to 1 week. Cookies may be frozen and recrisped for 5 minutes in 350° F oven. Preheat oven to 400° F before baking each batch of cookies.

Makes 7 dozen cookies.

Crystal sugar is sold with cookie- and cake-decorating items in supermarkets and specialty food stores. The sugar crystals are several times larger than granulated sugar crystals and are very shiny. Buy clear or colored crystal sugar. English coffee sugar is a pale brown color and comes in irregular chunks. Place it in a plastic bag and crush the chunks with a rolling pin or hammer until they are the size of crystal sugar.

Cookies make a perfect gift any time of year. From front to back: Orange Sand Cookies, Currant Butter Thins, Florentines, Financiers (in two shapes), Chocolate-Dipped Almond Meringue Batons, and Chocolate-Drizzled Hazelnut Cookies.

DIAMOND-STUDDED SUGAR COOKIES

These creamy sugar cookies are edged in sparkling crystal sugar. Make them plain or with pecans.

> ¾ cup unsalted butter, softened
> ½ cup sugar
> 2 cups flour
> 2 egg yolks, lightly beaten
> ½ cup crystal sugar (see page 117)

1. In medium bowl of electric mixer, cream butter and sugar together until light. Stir or cut flour into butter mixture with as few strokes as possible.

2. Divide dough into 3 equal portions. Form each portion into a ball and roll each ball into a log that is about 8 inches long and 1 inch in diameter. Try to keep dough very compact so no air spaces form inside the logs of dough. Wrap each log well and refrigerate until firm (2 hours).

Dough may be frozen at this point or stored for 1 to 2 days in refrigerator.

3. Preheat oven to 325° F. Brush each log of dough with egg yolk. Place crystal sugar on a sheet of waxed paper and roll logs in crystal sugar. Cut each log into ³⁄₈-inch slices and place rounds ¾ inch apart on parchment-lined baking sheets. Bake until underside is very pale brown (15 to 20 minutes). The top will still be very pale. Cool cookies on wire racks.

4. Store cool cookies in an airtight container for up to 2 weeks.

Makes 5 dozen cookies.

Diamond-Studded Pecan Cookies Substitute ½ cup finely ground pecans for ½ cup of the flour. Roll cookies in crystal sugar, finely chopped pecans, or crushed English coffee sugar.

ORANGE SAND COOKIES
Sablées

These golden, glazed orange cookies are a crisp, buttery cross between sweet tart pastry and shortbread. They are usually 3 to 4 inches in diameter. Make them smaller if you want to include them on a tray of petits fours.

⅔ cup sugar
¾ cup unsalted butter, softened
3 egg yolks
1 teaspoon vanilla extract
3 teaspoons very finely grated orange rind
½ teaspoon baking powder
1⅓ cups flour
2 egg yolks lightly beaten with 1 teaspoon cream or milk (egg wash)

1. In large bowl of electric mixer, cream sugar and butter together. Beat in egg yolks, vanilla, and orange rind.

2. Sift baking powder with flour and cut into butter mixture with pastry blender. When just mixed, gather into two balls. Flatten each slightly with side of hand, cover, and refrigerate for 1 hour or until firm. (Dough can be refrigerated up to 2 days or frozen up to 6 weeks.)

3. Preheat oven to 350° F. Lightly butter 2 baking sheets. Place dough on lightly floured work surface, flour rolling pin, and roll dough out ³⁄₁₆ inch thick. Roll out as for Sweet Tart Pastry (see page 72). Slide a thin metal spatula under dough to separate it from work surface. Cut cookies out with a 3-inch scallop-edged cookie cutter. Dip cutter in flour before cutting each cookie. Place cookies ¼ inch apart on prepared baking sheets. Dough or unbaked cookies can be frozen (see page 55). Allow cookies to thaw slightly before brushing them with egg wash and baking.

4. Brush top of cookies with egg wash twice. Using the back of a dinner fork, press a crosshatch design on cookies.

5. Bake until light golden brown on top and bottom (15 minutes). Cool on wire rack. Store in airtight container up to 2 weeks.

Makes 2 dozen cookies.

CHOCOLATE-DRIZZLED HAZELNUT COOKIES

When making these elegant cookies, handle the dough gently from start to finish and you'll be rewarded with the thinnest hazelnut wafers imaginable. Cookies may be finished in two different ways: Drizzle single cookies with thin chocolate lines, or sandwich raspberry jelly between two cookies and drizzle melted chocolate over the top.

⅔ cup unsalted butter, softened
⅓ cup sugar
½ teaspoon vanilla extract
1¼ cups flour, sifted
1¼ cups hazelnuts, skinned and finely ground (see page 67)
2 ounces semisweet chocolate
⅓ cup raspberry jelly (optional)

1. In large bowl of electric mixer, cream butter and sugar together until light. Add vanilla.

2. Stir or cut flour and ground hazelnuts into butter mixture, using as few strokes as possible. Divide dough in half to form two balls; flatten each slightly. Wrap and refrigerate for at least 1 hour. (Dough can be refrigerated for up to 2 days.)

3. Preheat oven to 350° F. Remove dough from refrigerator and allow it to warm up slightly if too firm to roll out. Place dough on lightly floured surface, flour rolling pin, and roll dough out ⅛ inch thick. Roll out as you would a pie crust (see page 58), reflouring work surface and rolling pin as necessary to prevent sticking. This is a very fragile dough that must be rolled out gently and handled with care.

4. Slide a narrow metal spatula under dough to separate it from the work surface. Cut cookies out with a 1¾-inch scallop-edged cookie cutter. Dip cutter in flour before cutting each cookie. Place cookies ¼ inch apart on ungreased baking sheets.

5. Bake until cookies begin to turn a very pale brown at the edges (8 to 10 minutes). Do not allow them to become fully brown or cookies will taste bitter. Cool on wire racks.

6. *To decorate cookies with chocolate:* Melt chocolate in top of double boiler. Allow chocolate to cool to 86° F. Place in a paper piping cone with a very fine tip (¹⁄₃₂-inch opening). (See page 21 for how to form a piping cone.) Place all cookies on a sheet of waxed paper. Drizzle chocolate lines back and forth across cookies, making an irregular line decoration on each. Allow chocolate to harden before storing cookies.

7. *For double-decker cookies:* Melt jelly over low heat until bubbly. Spread a thin layer of warm jelly on top of half of the cookies. Place a second cookie, smooth side up, on top of each. Drizzle cookies with chocolate.

Makes 6 dozen flat cookies or 3 dozen double-decker cookies.

FRESH FRUIT SORBETS

For a light finale, serve fresh fruit sorbet with a tray of beautifully arranged cookies and petits fours. Sorbet, also called sherbet, looks very appealing when served in oval scoops surrounded by attractively arranged berries or slices of fruit. Sorbet is made from fresh fruit purée, a sugar syrup, and lemon juice. It is only as good as the fruit you make it from, so choose fully ripe seasonal fruit whenever possible.

The following recipes are approximate formulas for poached pear and strawberry sorbets. You will have to sweeten your fruit purée to taste because the sugar content of fruit varies considerably at different times of the year. Vine- and tree-ripened fruit at the peak of its season will have more natural sweetness and need less sugar syrup than underripe or bland fruit. The addition of lemon juice balances the sugar and enhances the flavor of the fruit. If the sorbet is too soft, you added too much sugar syrup to the purée. If too little sugar syrup is added to the fruit purée, the sorbet will be too hard. Pulpy fruits, such as pears, strawberries, papayas, persimmons, peaches, and so forth, yield smooth, creamy sorbets.

PEAR SORBET

Fresh poached pears yield a smooth, creamy, white pear sorbet that tastes delicious with any of the cookies featured in this chapter.

- 2 *tablespoons lemon juice*
- 2½ *pounds fully ripe pears*
- 3⅓ *cups water*
- 2½ *cups sugar*
  Half a lemon, sliced
- 1 *vanilla bean, split in half lengthwise*
- ⅓ *cup water*
- ½ *cup superfine sugar (see Glossary, pages 122–123)*
- 1 *tablespoon strained lemon juice*

1. *To make the pear purée:* Stir the 2 tablespoons lemon juice into a large bowl of cold water. Peel each pear, remove core and seeds, cut in half lengthwise, and place in lemon water (this keeps pears white).

2. Combine the 3½ cups water and the 2½ cups sugar in a heavy saucepan large enough to hold all of the pears comfortably (about a 4½-quart capacity). Stir over medium heat until sugar dissolves and syrup comes to a boil. Reduce heat and add lemon slices, vanilla bean, and pears. Cover pears with a circle of parchment paper and simmer gently for 5 minutes. Turn pears over and simmer until tender when pierced with the tip of a sharp knife (5 to 10 minutes, depending on ripeness of pears).

3. Transfer pears to a bowl; cover with the syrup and cool. Remove pears from bowl with a slotted spoon; process to a smooth purée in food processor. Reserve and chill 1 cup of the poaching syrup. Remaining syrup can be reused for poaching or used to moisten a cake.

4. *To prepare the sorbet:* Combine the ⅓ cup water and the ½ cup sugar in a small saucepan; stir over medium heat until sugar dissolves and syrup comes to a boil. Cool to room temperature; refrigerate until cold.

5. In a medium bowl combine the 1 cup reserved poaching syrup, the 1 tablespoon lemon juice, and pear purée. Then add half of the cold sugar syrup. Taste and add more syrup if mixture is not sweet enough. With very ripe pears it may not be necessary to add all of the syrup. The mixture should taste sweet but not overwhelmingly so. Add more lemon juice if needed to enhance the flavor of pears.

6. Freeze in ice cream freezer according to manufacturer's instructions. Store in freezer in stainless steel or plastic container with a tight-fitting lid. Will keep up to 2 weeks.

Makes about 4 cups.

STRAWBERRY SORBET

Garnish with a few sliced strawberries and a sprig of fresh mint.

- 1½ *cups sugar*
- 1 *cup water*
- 3 *cups strained strawberry purée (2½ baskets)*
- 1 *tablespoon strained lemon juice*

1. Combine sugar and water in a saucepan; stir over medium heat until sugar dissolves and syrup comes to a boil. Cool to room temperature, then refrigerate until cold.

2. Stem, hull, and wash strawberries. Purée strawberries in food processor; strain through fine-meshed sieve to remove seeds. Measure out 3 cups purée. Chill well in refrigerator.

3. Stir three fourths of the cold sugar syrup into the purée; add lemon juice. Taste and add more syrup if necessary. (Very ripe, sweet berries will not need all of the syrup.)

4. Freeze in ice cream freezer according to manufacturer's instructions. Store in freezer in stainless steel or plastic container with a tight-fitting lid. Will keep up to 2 weeks.

Makes about 4 cups.

Strawberry and Pear Sorbets are served with (front to back) a Cigarette Russe, Chocolate-Dipped Almond Meringue Batons, and Diamond-Studded Sugar Cookies.

GLOSSARY OF COOKING TERMS AND INGREDIENTS

Almond extract See Extracts.

Almond paste A combination of blanched, powdered almonds, sugar, and egg whites ground to a fine paste that can be rolled out in sheets or molded to form decorations for pastry (see recipe, page 28).

Angelica See Candied fruit.

Armagnac A brandy from the Armagnac region of France.

Bake To cook by dry heat, usually in an oven.

Baking powder A leavening agent composed of sodium aluminum sulfate (alkaline ingredient) and calcium acid phosphate (acid ingredient). These two ingredients react with one another in the presence of liquid and heat to produce bubbles of carbon dioxide gas, which cause pastries to rise. The leavening action begins in the cold dough and continues even more forcefully in the oven (thus the term "double-acting"). Always use fresh baking powder (no more than three to four months old). Store in an airtight container.

Baking soda An alkaline substance, also called bicarbonate of soda, used to neutralize acid ingredients (such as molasses, sour cream, sour milk, buttermilk, honey, chocolate, and certain spices). This combination of alkaline with acid also produces carbon dioxide bubbles, which act as a leavening agent.

Batter A mixture of ingredients that can be poured or dropped from a spoon.

Beat To mix by stirring rapidly in a circular motion by hand or with electric mixer.

Blanch To drop briefly in boiling water to help loosen the skin (of almonds and peaches, for example) or to partially cook the ingredient.

Blanched almonds Almonds with skins removed (see page 67).

Blend To mix two or more ingredients together until smooth or until they combine to produce a uniform texture, color, or flavor.

Boil To heat a liquid to the boiling point (212° F at sea level). When it reaches the boiling point, all of the liquid will be in motion, with bubbles constantly rising and breaking on the surface.

Brown butter Nut-brown butter (*beurre noisette*) is butter that has been heated until golden brown.

Brush To lightly graze the surface of a pastry with a pastry brush, either to clean excess flour from dough or to apply a thin coat of glaze to the dough (such as egg wash, warm jelly, and so forth)

Butter To spread or brush a thin layer of soft or melted butter evenly over the inside surface of a pan or on parchment paper.

Butter and flour To spread a thin layer of butter on the inside of a pan and then coat the surface of the butter with a thin layer of flour.

Calvados Apple brandy from the Normandy region of France. American applejack can be substituted.

Candied fruit (glacé fruit) Fruits or parts of herbs preserved in sugar syrup. Used to decorate pastries or enhance taste of pastry.

Candied angelica Made from the stems of angelica, a plant with a slight licorice flavor. It resembles very green celery stalks when candied. Can be sliced and used to decorate cakes.

Candied citron Sometimes called cedro. A green, candied citrus-like peel that is cut up and used to decorate pastries or as an ingredient in fruitcakes.

Candied orange peel Used to flavor or decorate pastries.

Caramelize To cook sugar slowly until it melts and turns a deep, golden brown.

Carbon dioxide An odorless gas that can aerate a batter, causing it to rise.

Cardamom An aromatic spice whose seeds are used whole or ground. To grind seeds, remove them from their husk and grind with a mortar and pestle.

Cedro See Candied citron.

Chill To make something cold by placing it in the refrigerator or by stirring it over ice water.

Coat a spoon A term used to describe the consistency of a mixture when it has thickened enough to leave a thin film on the back of a spoon.

Combine To mix two or more ingredients until blended.

Comb scraper A metal or plastic triangle with serrated edges used to create patterns in icing or chocolate.

Core To remove the central part of a fruit (pears, apples).

Cream To beat a mixture of ingredients until they reach a soft, smooth consistency.

Cream of tartar An acid ingredient used to stabilize beaten egg whites. Not necessary if you beat the whites in a copper bowl.

Crème fraîche A French heavy cream that has a slightly tart taste and is about the consistency of American sour cream (see recipe, page 38).

Crystal sugar (candy sugar) Broken rock candy that looks like clear sugar crystals. Makes cookies and cakes sparkle.

Crystallized violets or roses Flower petals candied in sugar syrup. Used to decorate cakes.

Curdled A term used to describe a liquid that has separated into liquid and solid pieces (clumps); coagulated liquid.

Cut in To mix solid fat into dry ingredients using a cutting motion (with two knives or a pastry blender).

Docker An implement covered with spikes used to prick holes in pastry dough. A dinner fork can be used for the same purpose.

Dot To scatter small pieces of butter over the surface of something.

Drizzle To pour a liquid in a thin stream over a surface to create a pattern of irregularly spaced fine lines.

Dust To sprinkle a fine layer of a powder (such as flour, confectioners' sugar, or powdered nuts) over a surface.

Egg wash Egg or egg yolk lightly beaten with water. Used to give shiny surface to pastry or to glue two pieces of raw pastry together.

Extracts (lemon, orange, almond, etc.) Liquid flavorings used to perfume pastries. Use only extracts labeled "pure"—those made with an alcohol base. Add to cool mixtures for strongest effect.

Flour To dust the inside of a buttered mold with a fine layer of flour.

Fold To incorporate a light, aerated mixture into a heavier mixture without deflating the lighter mixture (see page 25 for technique).

Fondant An opaque white icing used to glaze cakes and pastries (see page 104).

Framboise A clear, raspberry-flavored French liqueur.

Gelatin Protein derived from the bones and connective tissues of animals. Usually available in granular (powdered) form or in sheets. Recipes in this book call for unflavored powdered gelatin. Soften 1 tablespoon gelatin in ¼ cup cold liquid. Then dissolve in hot liquid or stir over hot water until dissolved and add to 75° F liquid. One tablespoon gelatin will set 2 cups liquid when mixture is chilled 2 to 4 hours.

Génoise A sponge cake.

Ginger root The tuberous root of a lily (*Zingiber officinale*). Used to flavor pastry. Powdered ginger may be substituted (see chart, page 22).

Glaze To coat a surface with a thin layer of sugar, icing, chocolate, jelly, egg wash, and so on, to give it a shiny finish.

Gluten The elastic protein created when wheat flour is mixed with a liquid.

Grate To grind solid food against a metal object (grater) to produce shreds, flakes, or tiny particles.

Hull To remove the outer part of nuts. To remove stems and inner hard core from strawberries.

Hydrogenated vegetable shortening A vegetable oil that has had air incorporated into it, making it solidify and turn white. Can be stored at 70° F for a very long time.

Ice To spread a layer of frosting on a pastry.

Kirsch A European cherry-flavored brandy.

Knead To work dough with hands into a malleable mass by pressing and folding.

Lard Rendered pork fat. Store in refrigerator or cool place.

Line To cover the inside of a pan, or just the bottom of a pan, with a piece of parchment, foil, or waxed paper.

Macerate To place foods in a liquid so they will soften and absorb the liquid's flavors.

Mortar and pestle Consists of a bowl (the mortar) and a rounded stick (the pestle). Useful for grinding spices, nuts, and so forth. Mortar and pestle should be made of the same material (marble or porcelain are best).

Nutmeg (whole, freshly grated) The hard inner kernel (seed) of the fruit of a nutmeg tree (*Myristica fragrans*). Grate only the amount you need with a fine grater or nutmeg grinder.

Parchment paper (kitchen parchment) This nonstick paper is used to line baking sheets and pans. It is available in rolls or sheets at cookware stores. You can substitute aluminum foil, but parchment is far superior.

Pastry bags Useful sizes: 10-inch, 14-inch, 16-inch. Lightweight nylon bags are easy to use. Wash thoroughly in very hot, sudsy water after every use; rinse well and allow to dry completely before storing.

Pastry blender A hand-held tool with six curved wires used to cut shortening into flour when making dough for a pie or tart crust.

Pastry brushes Soft-bristle brushes used to apply glaze or egg wash to pastry or to brush flour from dough. Stock a variety of sizes from 1 to 3 inches wide. Smaller soft artists brushes are handy for decorating or glazing miniature pastries.

Pastry cutters Sets of cutters or individual cutters (metal) used to cut sheets of dough into different shapes. The sets are available in round, oval, or boat shapes, with plain or scalloped edges. Individual cookie cutters are sold in numerous sizes and shapes. Useful for cutting out dough to decorate pastries.

Peel To remove the rind or skin of a fruit.

Pie weights Small metal weights used in blind-baking pastry. Dried beans can also be used as pie weights.

Pipe To force a mixture through the opening of a pastry bag to create a decorative effect or give shape to the mixture.

Pit To remove the seed from a fruit (such as a peach, plum, or cherry).

Poach To cook gently in liquid that is barely simmering so the food being cooked retains its original shape.

Polenta A coarsely ground cornmeal.

Praline Powdered caramelized almonds and/or hazelnuts (see page 24).

Preheat To allow oven to heat to the desired temperature before placing pastry in oven (15 to 20 minutes).

Prick dough To pierce small holes all over dough with a docker, fork, or knife tip to allow steam to escape during baking.

Purée To blend, sieve, or process food into a soft, smooth consistency.

Ribbon A term used to describe the consistency of a batter or egg white mixture such as that used in meringue or génoise. When you lift the whisk from the bowl, the beaten mixture falls slowly from the whisk and leaves a ribbon trail on top of the mixture in bowl. It remains on top for a few seconds before sinking back into the rest of the mixture.

Rind The peel or skin of a fruit.

Rum A liquor made from cane sugar and used to flavor pastries.

Score To cut shallow lines partway through the top layer of dough to create a decorative pattern.

Sieve To strain liquids to separate small particles from larger ones.

Sift To pass a dry ingredient through a sieve or sifter to eliminate lumps or to separate large pieces from smaller ones.

Simmer To cook at just below the boiling point (about 180° F).

Stir To mix ingredients together with a spoon until well mixed. Use a slow, wide, circular motion; do not beat.

Strainer (sieve) Strainers are useful for separating out large pieces (such as separating seeds from juice or whole nuts from ground nuts).

For sifting flour: a single-screen medium wire strainer with a handle, or a wooden-frame, medium-mesh drum sieve (called a *tamie*). Avoid triple-layer sifters because they often clog and are difficult to clean.

For straining juices: a double-mesh, stainless steel, bowl-shaped strainer with handle.

Thermometers Three types are most useful in baking:

Candy thermometer: For temperatures up to 370° F or 400° F (depending on thermometer). Usually has markings indicating jelly stage, and soft-ball through hard-crack stages. Always warm thermometer in hot water before plunging it into boiling sugar syrup. Wash in in hot water immediately after using.

Instant-read thermometer: For temperatures less than 220° F. To test temperature of melted chocolate.

Oven thermometer: Use to check oven calibration for accuracy and check oven for hot spots.

Toast To toast nuts by baking them in oven until surface of nut turns light brown or until nut is crisp and dry (see page 67).

Toss To mix lightly by lifting and turning ingredients with fingertips, two forks, or two spoons.

Turn A term used in making puff pastry. A turn involves rolling dough into a rectangle, folding it into thirds like a business letter and, before rolling it out again, turning the dough clockwise a quarter turn.

Turn out To remove a baked pastry from the pan in which it was baked. Cakes and cupcakes are turned out by inverting baking pan over a wire cooling rack and lifting off the pan. To remove tarts from tins (with loose bottoms), push up the removable bottom and allow the sides of the tin to fall away from the tart. For tarts baked in a tart band, lift the ring off, then slide the tart onto a cooling rack.

Vanilla bean The pod of a climbing plant cultivated in Mexico and other tropical regions.

Vanilla extract A liquid flavoring used in baking, made by soaking (macerating) vanilla beans in a 35 percent alcohol solution. Use only extract, never imitation vanilla, which has artificial flavoring. Add to cool mixtures for strongest effect.

Vegetable shortening See Hydrogenated vegetable shortening.

Whip To beat rapidly in a circular motion in order to increase a mixture's volume by incorporating air into it. Accomplished with a whisk or whip attachment of electric mixer.

Whisk A wire utensil used to whip air into eggs, cream, or butter. To beat with a wire whisk.

Zester A tool used to remove rind (colored part of skin only) from citrus fruits.

INDEX

Note: Page numbers in italics refer to illustrations.

126

U.S. Measure and Metric Measure Conversion Chart

	Symbol	Formulas for Exact Measures: When you know:	Multiply by	To find:	Rounded Measures for Quick Reference		
Mass (Weight)	oz	ounces	28.35	grams	1 oz		= 30 g
	lb	pounds	0.45	kilograms	4 oz		= 115 g
	g	grams	0.035	ounces	8 oz		= 225 g
	kg	kilograms	2.2	pounds	16 oz	= 1 lb	= 450 g
					32 oz	= 2 lb	= 900 g
					36 oz	= 2¼ lb	= 1,000 g (1 kg)
Volume	tsp	teaspoons	5.0	milliliters	¼ tsp	= 1/24 oz	= 1 ml
	tbsp	tablespoons	15.0	milliliters	½ tsp	= 1/12 oz	= 2 ml
	fl oz	fluid ounces	29.57	milliliters	1 tsp	= 1/6 oz	= 5 ml
	c	cups	0.24	liters	1 tbsp	= ½ oz	= 15 ml
	pt	pints	0.47	liters	1 c	= 8 oz	= 250 ml
	qt	quarts	0.95	liters	2 c (1 pt)	= 16 oz	= 500 ml
	gal	gallons	3.785	liters	4 c (1 qt)	= 32 oz	= 1 l.
	ml	milliliters	0.034	fluid ounces	4 qt (1 gal)	= 128 oz	= 3¾ l.
Length	in.	inches	2.54	centimeters	⅜ in.	= 1 cm	
	ft	feet	30.48	centimeters	1 in.	= 2.5 cm	
	yd	yards	0.9144	meters	2 in.	= 5 cm	
	mi	miles	1.609	kilometers	2½ in.	= 6.5 cm	
	km	kilometers	0.621	miles	12 in. (1 ft)	= 30 cm	
	m	meters	1.094	yards	1 yd	= 90 cm	
	cm	centimeters	0.39	inches	100 ft	= 30 m	
					1 mi	= 1.6 km	
Temperature	° F	Fahrenheit	5/9 (after subtracting 32)	Celsius	32° F	= 0° C	
					68 °F	= 20° C	
	° C	Celsius	9/5 (then add 32)	Fahrenheit	212° F	= 100° C	
Area	in.^{2}	square inches	6.452	square centimeters	1 in.^{2}	= 6.5 cm^2	
	ft^2	square feet	929.0	square centimeters	1 ft^2	= 930 cm^2	
	yd^2	square yards	8,361.0	square centimeters	1 yd^2	= 8,360 cm^2	
	a	acres	0.4047	hectares	1 a	= 4,050 m^2	